A Game at Chess

THE NEW MERMAIDS

General Editors
PHILIP BROCKBANK
BRIAN MORRIS

A Game at Chess

THOMAS MIDDLETON

Edited by J. W. HARPER
Lecturer in English, York University

A New Mermaid

A MERMAID DRAMABOOK
HILL AND WANG • NEW YORK

Manufactured in the United States of America
1234567890

CONTENTS

ACKNOWLEDGEMENTS

CRITICAL STUDY of the textual problems of *A Game at Chess* really began with R. C. Bald's edition of 1929 and it is to Professor Bald's edition that all present day students of the play must be primarily indebted. His later articles on Middleton have also been used extensively in the present edition.

The work of the nineteenth century editors, Dyce and Bullen, has also been consulted and some of their notes used. The one other modern edition, that of C. F. Tucker Brooke and N. B. Paradise in their *English Drama, 1580–1642*, has provided many useful suggestions.

A number of articles on Middleton's play, such as those of Edgar C. Morris and John Robert Moore, have proved very valuable.

I should also like to thank the General Editors for their assistance.

ABBREVIATIONS USED IN NOTES

T = MS. 0. 2. 66. in the Library of Trinity College, Cambridge.
B = MS. E L 34 B. 17 in the Huntington Library.
L = MS. Lansdowne 690 in the British Museum.
M¦= MS. Malone 25 in the Bodleian Library.
F = MS. V. a. 342 in the Folger Library.
A = MS. V. A. 231 in the Folger Library.
Q1 = edition of 1625 (?), C. 34. 1. 23 in the British Museum.
Q2 = edition of 1625 (?), C. 34. d. 38 in the British Museum.
Q3 = edition of 1625 (?), C. 34. d. 37 in the British Museum.
Dyce = *The Works of Thomas Middleton*, ed. Alexander Dyce. 5 vols. (London, 1840).
Bald = Thomas Middleton, *A Game at Chesse*, ed. R. C. Bald (Cambridge, 1929).
Bullen = *The Works of Thomas Middleton*, ed. A. H. Bullen. 8 vols. (London, 1885–86).
Brooke and Paradise = Thomas Middleton, *A Game at Chess* in *English Drama, 1580–1642*, ed. C. F. Tucker Brooke and N. B. Paradise (New York, 1933).

INTRODUCTION

THE AUTHOR

THOMAS MIDDLETON was born in London in 1580. His father, a man of some substance, a 'citizen and brick-layer', died when Thomas was only five years old and his school and university studies were clearly pursued against a turbulent, litigious background of suits raised by his mother against his adventurer stepfather. Although he matriculated at Queen's College, Oxford, in 1598, he probably did not take a degree.

In 1597 he published his first work, *The Wisdom of Solomon Paraphrased* (described by Swinburne as 'a tideless and interminable sea of fruitless and inexhaustible drivel') followed by other pamphlets in prose and verse. By 1600 he was settled in London 'daylie accompaninge the players', and by 1603 Middleton, now married, was writing comedies for Henslowe and others.

Throughout the first ten or fifteen years of the century Middleton wrote many successful comedies and intrigues of town life. Such plays as *Michaelmas Term*, *A Trick to Catch the Old One* and *A Mad World my Masters* carry the familiar Middleton apparatus of sharpers and usurers, tradesmen and courtesans, rich widows and gallants on the make—a seamy picture of London life which, while it has affinities with Jonson's, is without the latter's strong moral sense. Many of Middleton's characters are vicious and his irony heartless, but in these plays are some of the funniest scenes in Jacobean comedy—as, for instance, the christening scene in *A Chaste Maid in Cheapside*.

Around twenty-five plays have been definitely attributed to Middleton. Collaboration with Webster, Dekker, Beaumont and Rowley helped to give variety to his output, e.g. *A Fair Quarrel*, in collaboration with Rowley, is a tragi-comedy of a very different outlook from his other plays, with its discussion of 'honour' and the ethics of duelling. There is, in fact, considerable variety in Middleton's output: comedies, tragi-comedies, pageants and masques for city occasions (he became City Chronologer in 1620), a political satire, *A Game at Chess*, which caused a furore and may have led to the author's imprisonment, and two great tragedies, *Women Beware Women* and *The Changeling*. He died in 1627.

THE PLAY

THE FIRST PERFORMANCES

A Game at Chess was the first long run in English theatrical history. In Middleton's day, as in Shakespeare's, the dramatic companies normally presented a different play each day; but *A Game at Chess* opened at the Globe on Friday, 6 August 1624 and continued for nine successive days (excluding Sundays), and the first two quartos followed the title with the phrase 'as it was acted nine days together at the Globe on the Bankside'. Undoubtedly the play could have continued much longer if it had not been suppressed by the authorities. 'There were more than three thousand persons there on the day that the audience was smallest,' according to the indignant testimony of the Spanish Ambassador, who added:

> There was such merriment, hubbub and applause that even if I had been many leagues away it would not have been possible for me not to have taken notice of it.[1]

And John Chamberlain wrote that the play was

> frequented by all sorts of people old and young, rich and poor, masters and servants, papists and puritans, wise men etc., churchmen and statesmen . . .[2]

Clearly Middleton had found the perfect formula for popular success.

But his example was not followed and *A Game at Chess* remains unique. The success of the play was obviously due to its being a transparent political allegory, fully in accord with popular opinion of the day concerning current relations between England and Spain. The Spanish monarchy and its most successful ambassador were held up to ridicule, the Roman Catholic Church was savagely satirized, and in the final scene the whole Spanish nation was consigned to hell. Such political allegory was very dangerous, and at a moment when England and Spain stood poised on the verge of war Middleton's audacious play created an international incident. The players doubtless knew that their time would be short; by choosing a moment when the King was away from London and playing the piece on successive days they made a huge profit. But on the tenth day of the 'nine days' wonder' the strong protests of the Spanish Ambassador had their effect: the theatre was closed by the Privy Council and the King's Men forbidden to act. The next day a warrant was issued for Middleton's arrest.

THE SOURCES

The technical reason for the arraignment of the King's Men before the Privy Council on 18 August was their flaunting of the order against representing any modern Christian king on the stage, and that the White King was James I and the Black King Philip IV of Spain must have been difficult to deny. But the protests of the Spanish Ambassador, Don Carlos Coloma, against 'the insolence of the players' were not concerned with a violation of the law.[3] The very sources from which the play was moulded were enough to arouse the Ambassador's anger, and what Middleton had done with these sources was even more offensive.

The literary sources of the play were a selection of pamphlets from the spate of anti-Catholic and anti-Spanish propaganda which poured from the presses during James's reign. The speed at which Middleton worked is suggested by the passages in *A Game at Chess* which are drawn almost verbatim from such pamphlets and by the nearness in date of some of these effusions to the production of the play. Thomas Scott's *Vox Populi* (1620), Thomas Robinson's *The Anatomie of the English Nunnerie at Lisbon* (1622), John Gee's *The Foote Out of the Snare* (1624), these tracts and others like them[4] heated the popular imagination, which they served almost as newspapers, by painting a lurid picture of a Roman Catholic plan for world domination in which Spanish diplomacy and the Jesuit order united to form the spearhead; and Middleton took over anecdotes, allusions, and whole passages from these tracts and brought them to life in the speeches of the characters in his living chess game.

The second principal source of *A Game at Chess* is an historical incident, the rash visit by Prince Charles and the Duke of Buckingham to Madrid in 1623 to conduct in person the negotiations for a marriage between the Prince and the Infanta Maria. Middleton took advantage of the great popular outburst of relief and rejoicing when the Prince returned without a Spanish bride, and it was easy for him to represent the frustrated end of the negotiations as a 'checkmate by discovery' by the White Knight (Charles) and the White Duke (Buckingham), i.e., a discovery of the perfidious design behind the Spanish negotiations, the intention of converting the future King of England to Roman Catholicism.

In the confused state of popular feeling about Spain and Rome, two of the most notorious public figures of the day were vaguely associated with the visit to Madrid as important players in the great Catholic chess game. The focus of Middleton's satirical attack was on the Count of Gondomar (the Black Knight), Spanish Ambassador in England until 1622 and one of Spain's most skilled diplomatists. Gondomar's personal peculiarities made him an easily identifiable figure. His famous fistula is cruelly mocked throughout the play and the players actually managed to acquire his well known litter and 'chair of ease' and thus 'they counterfeited his person to the life'.[5] Middleton's character-sketch is, of course, almost pure caricature,[6] but the verve and ebullience of the Black Knight do capture what was apparently a true characteristic of the man whom the public regarded as 'the mightiest Machiavel-politician'.

As an after-thought Middleton combined his satire of Gondomar with another amusing caricature: the Fat Bishop is Marco Antonio de Dominis, the former Archbishop of Spalatro. A theologian of considerable ability, de Dominis deserted the Church of Rome for that of England and received preferments from the King. Then when conditions in Italy seemed to have altered to his advantage, he returned to Rome in 1622. But his rather comic theological vacillations were of less concern to the English public than his grasping peevish nature and the severity with which he administered the Hospital of the Savoy when James made him its Master.[7] As Gondomar represented the Machiavellian politician, so the gross figure of de Dominis loomed in the popular mind as the symbol of a religion based upon self-interest and time-serving.

The historical figure behind the traitorous White King's Pawn has occasioned some controversy, for no one perfectly fits all of his characteristics; but the recent discovery of an early draft of the play suggests the reason for this confusion. The character was probably conceived merely as The Traitor, the betrayer of the English and the Protestant cause, and thus both the disgrace of the Earl of Bristol and the figure of Sir Toby Matthew, the son of the Archibishop of York who had turned Jesuit, contributed to his conception. Then in April, 1624, the impeachment of Lionel Cranfield, the Earl of Middlesex, began before the House of Lords, and Middleton, apparently already well on with his play, added some lines which associated the White King's Pawn with the former Lord Treasurer. This Pawn—and we may remember Bacon's remark in the *Apologie*, that 'a Pawn before the King is ever much played upon'—is thus a composite figure, a polyhedron whose facets flash forth a multitude of contemporary faces.

It has been suggested[8] that the subplot, the conspiracy against the White Queen's Pawn, also has an historical source, that it is an allegory of the Thirty Years' War, specifically of the seizure of the Palatinate. Professor Bald rejected this theory completely and saw the subplot as a general indictment of the Jesuits in their pursuit of the individual Protestant soul. But good allegory produces this sort of uncertainty. It is not a mere point-for-point translation of one story into the terms of another but partakes of the qualities of symbolism. Its figures may suggest now one thing, now another, and its essence remains shifting and ambiguous.

Thus the sources of the most successful play of the Jacobean theatre were numerous: the political and religious propaganda of the day, contemporary diplomacy, the personalities of several notorious figures, perhaps even the political scene on the Continent; and the most important source of all was current public opinion. But for all that is known about the background of *A Game at Chess*, Middleton's play retains its element of mystery. Was 'the insolence of the players' entirely due to monetary considerations, or was *A Game at Chess* itself a move in the great game which it allegorized? Why did the censor, Sir Henry Herbert, ever license such an obviously dangerous play? And why, once the play had been licensed on 12 June 1624, did two months elapse before its first performance? Professor Dover Wilson has suggested[9] that Herbert must have been certain of approval in high places before issuing such a risky licence, and that since the play was fully in accord with the aims of those who were urging a war with Spain, notably Charles and Buckingham, the figure behind the players' daring may well have been the Duke of Buckingham himself. If so, the two months prior to the first public production may have been taken up with private performances at the instigation of 'the war party'. On the other hand, the treatment of Buckingham in the play is ambivalent; the fulsome praise accorded to the 'fair structure of comely honour' seems to be undercut by other passages which glance satirically at notorious weaknesses of the newly-created Duke. Middleton's chess play, like other great examples of the Royal Game, defies complete analysis. It is impossible to tell the players from the play.

THE PLAY

As a work of dramatic art *A Game at Chess* has never received its due recognition. Just as there has apparently been no public performance since the afternoon of 16 August 1624, so there is no history of criticism devoted to this play, though Swinburne did pause in the course of his essay on Middleton to call it 'one of the most complete and exquisite works of artistic ingenuity and dexterity that ever excited or offended, enraptured or scandalized an audience of friends or enemies', and in our own day T. S. Eliot has briefly commended it as 'a perfect piece of literary political art'.[10] No doubt the very thing which was mainly responsible for the play's momentary celebrity, its reliance upon allegorical representation of current political events, has caused its subsequent neglect. Today it is difficult to feel much excitement at the outcome of the negotiations for the Spanish marriage or much amusement at the sight of Count Gondomar seated in his 'chair of ease'. Middleton's problem was that of any artist who capitalizes on current events: can a work aimed at the audience of the moment be so constructed that it will retain the really essential part of its value? With the passing of interest in the events which Middleton allegorized the play's appeal depends upon the success with which a living chess game is made into drama.

That success will be seen to be considerable if we grasp the unique quality of this play. Middleton, as usual, remains the invisible author, making his own presence felt only in the power of the language and in the suave movement of the verse:

> But the heart, the heart, lady;
> So meek that as you see good Charity pictured still
> With young ones in her arms, so will he cherish
> All his young tractable sweet obedient daughters
> E'en in his bosom, in his own dear bosom.

But in viewing the play as a whole one becomes conscious of a powerful controlling hand behind it; for even though its form is compounded of many elements, it is one of the most perfectly unified dramas of the Jacobean theatre. The subplot of the attack on the White Queen's Pawn is completely integrated with the main action, the Black Knight's pursuit of 'the great existence, The hope monarchical'; and when the Knight confesses his own inability to see the connection, the Jesuit replies with finality:

> You may deny so
> A dial's motion, 'cause you cannot see
> The hand move, or a wind that rends the cedar.

At moments one completely loses consciousness of the political sources of the action and observes it merely as action, as a perfectly plotted dramatic spectacle; and the principal reason for Middleton's success in creating this unified dramatic image is the skill with which he uses the allegorical device of the chess game.

Why a game at chess? The work itself suggests that Middleton was a player of some skill. Thirteen years earlier Shakespeare had shown Ferdinand and Miranda at the culmination of their happiness on their magic island engaged in the Royal Game, and later the King's Men had presented two other plays in which Italians or Spaniards had been shown immersed in chess, *The Spanish Curate* and Middleton's *Women Beware Women* (both in 1622). Greco, the greatest chess master of the seventeenth century, had lived in London from 1622–24 and Middleton had probably seen him playing in the London ordinaries.[11] The English mind of the 1620's would doubtless have viewed chess as a current fad at court but primarily as the game of the Spanish and the Italians and its reliance upon subtle calculation made it the perfect metaphor for the complex political game which the Catholic powers were waging against the

Protestant. One of the recent historians of Renaissance diplomacy has adopted Middleton's title, and even some of his imagery, for his account of the great diplomatic duel between England and Spain: 'The Game at Chess'.[12]

Far more than any other writer who has used chess as an allegorical device, Middleton actually made his dramatic chess game approximate to real play. The moves of the pieces in the opening of this allegory of the negotiations for the Spanish marriage constitute a sort of visual pun: the game begins as a Queen's Gambit Declined.[13] The ending is likewise a punning reference to the denouement of the Spanish negotiations as it appeared to the English people: 'discovered mate', discovery of the Catholic grand design for a 'universal monarchy'. And even though such literalism is not aimed at elsewhere in the play, the work as a whole uses the chess game as an extended metaphor and the nature of that metaphor colours everything in it. Thus the allegory has two levels in the sense that behind the player who appears on the stage we see first a chessman and secondly a real person or quality, but in recognizing that person or quality we do not lose sight of the chessman. Every speech, every action seems, therefore, to be determined by two interacting forces, the powers of the particular pieces and the master plan.

But whose master plan? James I and Philip IV are themselves pieces in the game. The Pope is a chessman whose power is felt at a distance, even if he never appears on the segment of the board which we see. Nor does one really have the sense that the master plan is the author's: he is, after all, attempting to present history, something of which he himself is a part. And if the tradition of Middleton's imprisonment for this work and his release after a rhyming petition to the King is true, it would seem that he took his chess metaphor so seriously that, with his usual sardonic disillusionment, he saw himself as a piece rather than a player; for what he wrote to James was apparently this:

> A harmless game raised merely for delight
> Was lately played by the Black House and White.
> The White House won, but now the Black side brag
> They changed the game and put me in the bag;
> And, that which makes malicious joy more sweet,
> I lie now under hatches in the Fleet.
> Yet use your royal hand, my hopes are free;
> 'Tis but removing of one man, that's me.[14]

The play is an elaboration of a metaphor taken literally: human life *is* a chess game, and all men, whether Kings, Bishops, or Pawns with a gift for the drama, are but 'shapes and pieces of the game'.

Thus the dominant word in the language of the play is 'game'.

Again and again this word appears as Middleton rings the changes on all of its possible meanings. Sometimes it means game in the sense of object of pursuit; at others one's 'game' is one's role or job. When the Black Knight refers to the Prince's 'sweet game of youth', the word is used as a metaphor for a period of life and thus for a state of being. Generally, of course, it is used in the literal sense of chess game, but when so used it carries the implication of the great game of diplomatic chess which dominated the world in Middleton's day and, behind that, the forces which had set that game in motion. The eventual result of the interplay of these divergent yet interrelated meanings is that the play itself becomes one sustained metaphor: the game of life.

The Black Knight, the one great comic character of the work, dominates every scene in which he appears precisely because he is the supreme gamester. Here Middleton's allegorical technique is perfect: the well-known machinations of Gondomar are embodied in a character who perfectly embodies the leaping deviousness which characterizes the Knight's move. The Black Knight cynically enjoys the game, enjoys it too much; he is a chessman so intoxicated by the intricate possibilities open to him that he plays for the sake of the play rather than for victory. He can reply, when the Black King plots against the White Queen,

> You're too hot, sir,
> If she were took, the game would be ours quickly.

He does not really desire a final victory, for that would mean the end of the play; and he does not fear defeat because, like Odysseus, he is never at a loss.

The Black Knight is a character in the mould of Jonson's great overreachers and the culmination of the long line of 'Machiavel-politicians' in the Renaissance theatre. He is a worthy descendant of Marlowe's Barabas. In his torrential monologues the pamphlet literature of religious controversy, where so much of the linguistic vigour of the English Renaissance is found, flows into supple blank verse. His great paean to abstemiousness, which is simultaneously a gluttonous praise of gluttony, is the comic climax of the play, and in his gloating descriptions of his schemes past, present, and future his game becomes play with language:

> . . . in the large feast of our vast ambition
> We count but the White Kingdom whence you came from
> The garden for our cook to pick his salads;
> The food's lean France larded with Germany,
> Before which comes the grave chaste signiory
> Of Venice, served in capon-like in whitebroth;

From our chief oven, Italy, the bake-meats,
Savoy the salt, Geneva the chipped manchet;
Below the salt the Netherlands are placed,
A common dish at lower end o' the table
For meaner pride to fall to; for our second course
A spit of Portugals served in for plovers,
Indians and Moors for blackbirds; all this while
Holland stands ready melted, to make sauce
On all occasions; when the voider comes
And with such cheer our crammed hopes we suffice,
Zealand says grace, for fashion; then we rise.

Such exuberance characterizes everything that he does. The
Machiavellian who can meet the cry, 'Your plot's discovered' with

Which of the twenty thousand and nine hundred
Four score and five, canst tell?

is impossible to dislike. Did Middleton really prefer Gondomar's
dull White counterpart to this spirit too fiery for hell to hold, or was
the creation of the Black Knight the tribute of one lover of chess to
another? In any event, it is obvious that in creating the Black Knight
Middleton moved directly contrary to the general trend of the
theatre of his day. Whereas Shakespeare took the stock types of the
Vice and the *Miles Gloriosus* and, in Falstaff, moulded them into a
man, Middleton took a man, Gondomar, and reduced him to a stock
type. The result of this distillation is an unusual flavour: one recog-
nizes in the Black Knight not the stock 'Machiavel-politician' but a
caricature of this caricature, a good-humoured monster who retains
something of the familiar taint of humanity.

This deliberate abandonment of any effort at realistic characterization is seen throughout *A Game at Chess*, and indeed most of the
expectations with which we ordinarily approach the Jacobean drama
must be abandoned when we confront this play. There is no effort
at psychological analysis or subtle revelation of motive, for chessmen
move according to the rules of the game rather than by a completely
free choice of their own destinies. The impatience that one would feel
in another play with the pompous moralizing of the White King is
here dispelled by Middleton's underlying point: the English
Solomon is himself merely a piece in the game. That half of the
characters are unspotted images of virtue and the other half in-
credibly wicked is inevitable, given Middleton's dominant metaphor:
for the duration of the game the chess player does see the world in
terms of Black and White. But it may be rather confusing to reflect
that the really memorable scenes and characters in the play are those
associated with the Black House while the White pieces are merely
flat and dull. One remembers not only the Black Knight and the Fat

Bishop but the worried Black Knight's Pawn who has managed to commit a sin which even the *Taxae Sacrae Poenitentiariae* cannot absolve and the mischievous Black Queen's Pawn who out-jesuits the Jesuit. Occasionally one may be tempted to think that what Middleton is really presenting here is an amused caricature of the popular attitude.

This, however, is surely not the case and experiencing the work as a whole leaves a very different impression. The play is, after all, a satire and a satire of a very unusual sort. Here Swinburne's description is very much to the point. *A Game at Chess*, he wrote, is

> the only work of English poetry which may properly be called Aristophanic. It has the same depth of comic seriousness, the same earnest ardour and devotion to the old cause of the old country, the same solid fervour of enthusiasm and indignation which animated the third great poet of Athens against the corruption of art by the sophistry of Euripides and the corruption of manhood by the sophistry of Socrates.[15]

Swinburne is, as usual, both extravagant and astute; the parallel is by no means perfect, yet it is worth pondering. In Middleton's play, of course, the norm, the 'civic seriousness' of 'devotion to the old cause of the old country', is not represented by anyone like the Aeschylus of *The Frogs* or by such a brilliantly conceived character as the Strepsiades of *The Clouds*, but by the incredible innocence of the White Queen's Pawn and the tedious sententiousness of the White King. But the historical situation in which Middleton wrote placed him in the ideal position for a satirist and the technique which he adopted solved, as no other could have done, the difficulties with which satire confronts its practitioner. He had no need to create a character to serve as the convincing embodiment of a norm because he did not confront the satirist's usual problem, to persuade his audience that his view of things is right. Middleton's audience was with him from the beginning; in fact, from long before the beginning. And then too, that other perennial problem of the satirist, to prevent any reflection on the part of the audience that a drastic simplification of the issues is occurring, that there is much to be said for the other side, scarcely arises here because of Middleton's use of the chess-game metaphor. He creates a world of sheer fantasy and then, like all good writers of fantasy, proceeds to show us that his fantastic world is more real than the 'real' world since it is a revelation of our world's underlying laws. Once we have accepted Middleton's dominant metaphor he has obtained that 'absolute dominion over the minds of the spectators' which Dryden found essential to any non-realistic dramatic form.[16] After all, most chess problems are like most tragedies and comedies, most autobiographies, and most works of philosophy and history in that they are demonstrations of the proposition that White, surprisingly, is to play and win. Thus Middleton can treat his adversaries with good-humoured amusement, knowing that his audience detests them already and that the form of the play prevents their being taken seriously.

But the author of *A Game at Chess* did have to overcome the two most serious objections that satire can evoke: it is all too often brutally personal or purely destructive and negative, or both. A very large proportion of this play is devoted to the annihilation of Count Gondomar and the Archbishop of Spalatro, much of it to cruel mockery of their physical defects; and the lessening of our vital interest in these characters combined with the increase of our knowledge of them may remind us of Dryden's admission that the satirist has no right to the reputations of other men. But because he was allegorizing an historical situation, it was inevitable, of course, that Middleton's satire should be personal; and he could offer the most convincing apology available to the writer of personal satire, that his censure was a means of making up for deficiencies in human laws since it was directed at those who were above the law:

> That Black Knight
> Will never take an answer, 'tis a victory
> To make him understand he does amiss
> When he knows, in his own clear understanding
> That he does nothing else.

Then too, it is possible to make a better defence than this for the personal satire in *A Game at Chess*. It is not a purely destructive attack on notorious contemporaries. The play has a positive theme.

This can best be seen by considering what is surely the most important aspect of *A Game at Chess*. This play is not merely a move in the political chess game and an example of satire; above all it is spectacle. It is a sequence of converging and diverging shapes and colours, a pattern that unfolds before the eyes. To create the hybrid form of this play Middleton looked away from the commercial theatre of the 1620's and back to the past, to the roots of the English drama. He not merely adopted the allegorical convention of the medieval morality with its flat characterization and its world of black and white but also returned to the spirit of the drama of Lyly, and behind Lyly to the academic *Commedia Euridita*, itself based on classical models, with its highly formalized plot and characters and its symbolic stage where separate 'houses' indicated the location of each group of characters. The result is a form more closely akin to the masque than to the genres which were currently popular in the commercial theatre. In the place of intricate psychological analysis and a complex plot spun out of the interaction of conflicting psyches Middleton presents simple characters confronting each other with formal speeches and the masque-like spectacle of contrasting colours in movement.

> See 'em anon, and mark 'em in their play,
> Observe, as in a dance, they glide away.

These lines from the Induction which accompany our first sight of the pieces' movement across the board, are a perfect description of what follows. The stage directions suggest that the play made use of the music and formalized movement of the masque to an unusual degree, and Middleton's experience as City Chronologer doubtless gave him valuable experience in the staging of a play which inclined so much toward spectacle.[17] The mingling of contemporary politics and the vivacious caricatures of Gondomar and de Dominis with this stately ceremonial gives *A Game at Chess* its unique quality, a flavour to which no other play has ever approximated.

Now if we attend to the play as spectacle, as an unfolding pattern, we shall find that the total pattern, as is often the case with intricate designs, creates its final unity out of diverse elements. As well as being contrasted in colour, the White and the Black sides move in different ways; they are performing different sorts of dance. This is what *A Game at Chess* is finally designed to show.

The Black House is thoroughly disunited. Not only are its men incapable of co-operation, their interests constantly conflict. Middleton's version of Jesuit ethics placed in the mouth of Ignatius Loyola in the Induction, forecasts what ensues:

> Pawns argue but poor spirits, and slight preferments,
> Not worthy of the name of my disciples.
> If I had stood so nigh, I would have cut
> That Bishop's throat but I'd have had his place
> And told the Queen a love-tale in her ear
> Would make her best pulse dance.

Which provokes Error's protest:

> Why, would you have 'em play against themselves?
> That's quite against the rule of game, Ignatius.

This is exactly what the Black pieces do, play against themselves. The Black Knight and the Black King disagree over strategy, each preferring his own form of sport, and the Black Knight attacks the Fat Bishop not to benefit the side but for revenge. The Black Knight's Pawn, who has made a blunder which he wishes to retract, is merely jeered at by his fellows. The Black Bishop's Pawn places his own pleasure before his King, and the game and he is betrayed by the

Black Queen's Pawn because he has formerly betrayed her. The Black House can draw together only when facing imminent and obvious disaster (as at II, i), and then only momentarily. And the final scene is the epitome of all that has preceded, 'contention in the pit' as the condemned pieces battle for the best seat in hell. The motivating principle of all the Black pieces is, of course, that stated by Ignatius in the Induction: 'Push, I would rule myself, not observe rule.' The dance of the Black House is like that of Comus's Rout.

The White pieces move according to an altogether different pattern. Apart from the traitorous King's Pawn, who proves to be a Black piece in disguise, they illustrate perfect co-operation and interdependence. The Pawns support each other (III, ii). The White Bishop rescues the menaced White Queen and the King moves up to assist them. The White Knight, Duke, and Bishop's Pawn unite in a manoeuvre to save the White Queen's Pawn; and in the finale the discovered mate is 'the noblest mate of all' presumably because it depends upon the perfect co-ordination of two pieces. The White side win because they move together in perfect harmony.

Middleton's chess lesson is valuable. Players must observe the same rules, but they need not use the possibilities created by these rules in the same way and the mark of the tyro is the chaos which he manages to create amongst his own ranks. Even if life is a game of chess we can play it well or ill, and Middleton's play presents a perfectly sound political philosophy in a dramatic image. If we attend to the spectacle presented by *A Game at Chess*, to the contrasting patterns which gradually emerge from this ballet on the sixty-four squares of the world, what the play eventually creates is a vision of two contrasting societies. One of them is a collection of individuals, united only by the accidents of circumstance, each pursuing his own narrow ends and motivated by the desire to rule himself, not observe rule. The other is a harmonious whole which derives its unity and power from the ability of each of its members to perform the function for which he is best fitted and to subordinate his own interests to a common end; and no society can do this, of course, unless its members are moved by a common spirit. This is what Middleton has really allegorized in *A Game at Chess* and what remains in the patterned movement of the spectacle long after the personal foibles of Gondomar and de Dominis have been forgotten: the contrast between a society which fulfils Plato's description of utopia in *The Republic*, which is just and powerful because it is based upon effective co-ordination, and a society which is in every respect the opposite.

There is no reason to suppose that Middleton, 'the most veritable realist of his age' as Schelling called him, seriously believed himself to be presenting an accurate picture of the English, as opposed to the Spanish, society of his era as they could be observed in day-to-day life; but it is not, of course, the primary business of art to provide a mere reflection of reality. And very probably the underlying conception of this play was based upon something which its author had actually witnessed. Middleton was eight years old when the Spanish Armada was defeated; he was twenty-five when the national rejoicing over the discovery of the Gunpowder Plot occurred; and just ten months before the first public performance of *A Game at Chess* the Prince of Wales returned from his dangerous journey to Madrid. When Prince Charles and his companion reached London on 6 October 1623 they were greeted with an outburst of national enthusiasm such as has seldom been witnessed in the history of any country. 'Never before,' writes Gardiner, 'had rejoicing so universal and so spontaneous been known in England.'[18] The bells sounded and the cannon roared a welcome. The Strand was so choked with people shouting 'Long live the Prince of Wales' that the royal carriage could scarcely pass. Wealthy citizens gave banquets in the streets for all comers and debtors were released from prison by anonymous benefactors: in an instant the economic and social divisions of the world of London were swept away. Candles were lighted in the windows at night and the sky was red with bonfires; and at St. Paul's an anthem was sung from the 114th Psalm: 'When Israel came out of Egypt, and the house of Jacob from amongst the barbarous people.' For a moment the nation must have seemed completely united, and the common spirit of a people, usually hidden beneath a welter of conflicting interests, was made a visible reality. For a moment it must have made sense to speak, in Swinburne's words about Aristophanes, of 'the old cause of the old country'. And then the moment passed.

It is not known at exactly what time, during the ensuing eight months, *A Game at Chess* was written, but surely there can be no doubt about the moment when the essence of the play was conceived. What remained, after that week in October, was to find a form sufficient to convey Middleton's disillusioned view of life, his amused contempt for the enemies of his country, and his sense of the national spirit which would render those enemies futile. The play which had to be written would not be an attempt to present a realistic picture of what was, but a work of the sort which Sidney might have approved: a vision which, in embodying in a dramatic metaphor the great ideal of national harmony, was a vision of what might and ought to be.

NOTE ON THE TEXT

A GAME AT CHESS is unique among Jacobean plays in that it exists in many more contemporary manuscripts than printed texts. The number of manuscripts is clearly due to the immense popularity of the play combined with its suppression: there was naturally a great demand for texts which the printers were forbidden to supply. Six manuscripts have now been discovered as against three quartos.

The play is also unusual in that, as R. C. Bald has demonstrated in his edition, one of the manuscripts, that at Trinity College, Cambridge, is in Middleton's own hand. Still another, the Bridgewater manuscript in the Huntington Library, is partially in the author's hand. Two other manuscripts, the Lansdowne manuscript in the British Museum and the Malone manuscript in the Bodleian Library (which presents an abridged version of the play) are in the hand of Ralph Crane the scrivener.

Professor Bald also pointed out that the first two quartos were derived from manuscripts similar to the Trinity and Bridgewater-Huntington manuscripts, those supervised by the author, while Q3 is much closer to the manuscripts transcribed by Crane.

Since the publication of Bald's edition two other manuscripts have come to light. The first of these, in the Folger Library, (v.a. 342) is the work of two scribes, is related to both of the two groups into which the other texts fall, and contains a great many errors. Its principal interest is that it is the only manuscript which offers as full a version of the text as is to be found in the quartos.

The other new discovery is of considerable interest. Once owned by the eighteenth century Irish antiquary, Mervyn Archdale, this manuscript (also in the Folger Library: v.a. 231) is dated 13 August 1624, thus in the middle of the play's brief run, and presents what is obviously an early version of the play. Many passages which are found in all the other texts are omitted, the character of the Fat Bishop is absent altogether, and the lines which most closely associated the White King's Pawn with the Earl of Middlesex are likewise missing. The Archdale manuscript shows that Middleton's conception of the play changed as he decided to include de Dominis and the Lord Treasurer in his satire.

Since the Trinity manuscript is Middleton's own, it has been taken as the copy-text. Where the Trinity manuscript omits passages present in other versions thay have been supplied wherever possible from the Bridgewater-Huntington manuscript.

But even though the author's manuscript possesses great authority as a copy-text, the Trinity manuscript presents certain editorial problems. It contains a few obvious errors which reference to the other texts can correct. Its lineation is occasionally curiously awry, and attention is called in the notes to the places where this has been set right by reference to other texts. And finally, Middleton's punctuation is often careless and worse than useless as a guide to the delivery of the verse. I have followed it wherever possible but have often been obliged to modify it for ease in reading.

I have indicated only those variants from the other texts which alter or emend the Trinity manuscript, but have called attention to all of the significant omissions and variants of the Archdale manuscript so that Middleton's original conception of the play can be grasped.

Spelling and capitalization have been modernized and the Latin stage directions of the manuscript translated. Scene divisions have been supplied from the Lansdowne manuscript and from Q3.

FURTHER READING

Bald, R. C. 'A New Manuscript of Middleton's *Game at Chesse*'. *Modern Language Review*, xxv (1930), 474–478.

Bald, R. C. 'An Early Version of Middleton's *Game at Chesse*'. *Modern Language Review*, xxxviii (1943), 177–80.

Eliot, T. S. 'Thomas Middleton'. *Selected Essays*. 3rd Edition (London, 1951).

Moore, John Robert. 'The Contemporary Significance of Middleton's *Game at Chesse*'. *PMLA*, L (1935), 761–768.

Morris, Edgar C. 'The Allegory in Middleton's *A Game at Chess*'. *Englische Studien*, XXXVIII (1907), 39–52.

Swinburne, Algernon Charles. Introduction to *Thomas Middleton* (Mermaid Series), ed. Havelock Ellis, I (London, 1887), vii–xxxviii.

Wilson, Edward M. and Olga Turner. 'The Spanish Protest Against *A Game at Chesse*'. *Modern Language Review*, XLIV (1949), 476–482.

Wilson, J. Dover. [Review of R. C. Bald's edition] *The Library*, Fourth Series, XI (1930), 105–116.

NOTES

1. Edward M. Wilson and Olga Turner, 'The Spanish Protest Against *A Game at Chesse*', *Modern Language Review*, XLIV (1949), 480.

2. *The Letters of John Chamberlain*, ed. N. E. McClure (Philadelphia, 1939), II, 578.

3. Wilson and Turner, *ibid.*, p. 476.

4. For a discussion of all the possible sources see Thomas Middleton, *A Game at Chesse*, ed. R. C. Bald (Cambridge, 1929), pp. 13–16. The only source which has been definitely identified since 1929 is the anonymous pamphlet *A Jesuites Oration to the Prince* (1623).

5. *The Letters of John Chamberlain, loc. cit.*

6. For a modern historian's view of the true nature of Gondomar's activities see Charles H. Carter, 'Gondomar: Ambassador to James I', *Historical Journal*, VII (1964), 189–208.

7. See the anonymous pamphlet *Newes from Rome: Spalato's Doome* (1624).

8. Edgar C. Morris, 'The Allegory in Middleton's *A Game at Chesse*', *Englische Studien*, XXXVIII (1907), 39–52.

9. J. Dover Wilson, [Review of R. C. Bald's edition] *The Library*, Fourth Series, XI (1930), 110–112.

10. Algernon Charles Swinburne, Introduction to *Thomas Middleton* (Mermaid Series), ed. Havelock Ellis, I (London, 1887), xxiii; T. S. Eliot, 'Thomas Middleton', *Selected Essays*, 3rd edition (London, 1951), p. 166.

11. John Robert Moore, 'The Contemporary Significance of Middleton's *Game at Chesse*', *PMLA*, L (1935), 764–765.

12. Garrett Mattingly, *Renaissance Diplomacy* (London, 1962), Chapter XXVI.

13. Moore, *ibid.*, pp. 765–766.

14. Four versions of this poem have now been discovered. See Geoffrey Bullough, '*The Game at Chesse*: How it Struck a Contemporary', *Modern Language Review*, XLIX (1954), 163.

15. Swinburne, *loc. cit.*

16. *Essays of John Dryden*, ed. W. P. Ker (Oxford, 1900), I, 155.

17. See R. C. Bald, 'Middleton's Civic Employments', *Modern Philology*, XXXI (1933), 76–78.

18. S. R. Gardiner, *History of England*, V (London, 1908), 129.

A GAME at CHESSE.

by T. Middleton

The title page, in Thomas Middleton's hand, of the Trinity Manuscript
in the library of Trinity College, Cambridge

[Dramatis Personae

White King	Black King
White Knight	Black Knight
White Duke	Black Duke
White Bishop	Black Bishop
White Pawns	Black Pawns

Fat Bishop
Fat Bishop's Pawn

White Queen	Black Queen
White Queen's Pawn	Black Queen's Pawn

IN THE INDUCTION

Ignatius Loyola
Error]

A GAME AT CHESS

Prologue

What of the game called chess-play can be made
To make a stage-play shall this day be played.
First you shall see the men in order set,
States and their Pawns, when both the sides are met,
The Houses well distinguished; in the game   5
Some men entrapped and taken, to their shame,
Rewarded by their play, and in the close
You shall see check-mate given to virtue's foes.
But the fairest jewel that our hopes can deck
Is so to play our game to avoid your check.   10

The Induction

IGNATIUS LOYOLA *appearing*, ERROR *at his foot as asleep*

IGNATIUS
    Hah! Where? What angle of the world is this,
That I can neither see the politic face
Nor with my refined nostrils taste the footsteps
Of any of my disciples, sons and heirs
As well of my designs as institutions?   5
I thought they'd spread over the world by this time,
Covered the earth's face and made dark the land
Like the Egyptian grasshoppers.
Here's too much light appears shot from the eyes
Of truth and goodness never yet deflowered;   10
Sure they were never here. Then is their monarchy
Unperfect yet, a just reward I see

4 *States* the pieces as distinct from pawns
3 *taste* scent, detect

Omitted in M, F, A. In L the Prologue follows the Induction.
s.d. *Ignatius Loyola* (1491–1556). Founder of the Society of Jesus, or
    Jesuit Order.
  8 *Egyptian grasshoppers.* The metaphor of a swarm of insects was com-
    monly applied to the Jesuits in the anti-Catholic pamphlets of the day.
    Cf. III.i, 88–98.

5

For their ingratitude so long to me,
Their father and their founder.
'Tis not five years since I was sainted by 'em,   15
Where slept my honour all the time before?
Could they be so forgetful to canonize
Their prosperous institutor? When they had sainted me
They found no room in all their calendar
To place my name that should have removed princes,   20
Pulled the most eminent prelates by the roots up
For my dear coming to make way for me,
Let every petty martyr and saint homily,
Roch, Maine, and Petronill, itch- and ague-curers,
Your Abbess Aldegund, and Cunegund,   25
The widow Marcell, parson Polycarp,
Cecily and Ursula, all take place of me,
And but for the bisextile, or leap-year,
And that's but one in three, I fall by chance

---

23 *Let* Q3 (T omits)
27 *Cecily and Ursula* ed. Sislie and Vrslie T

---

15 Loyola's Beatification was pronounced by Paul V in 1609; the Bull for
   his canonization was published by Urban VIII on 6 August 1623.
24 St. Roch (1295–1378) and St. Maine (or Mewan, d. 617) are associated
   with the healing of the sick. It is not certain which St. Petronilla is
   referred to.
      Bald (pp. 137–138) cites the passage which obviously inspired this
   line: 'What particular office hath father Ignatius? or what part is there
   commonly assigned vnto him for the succour of men? for I make no
   doubt, but as God hath assigned to every orher [*sic*] Saint the cure of
   some one disease or other, as to St. *Roch* the plague, to St. *Petronel* the
   feuer, to St. *Main* the itch, so St. *Ignatius* hath some certain one vnto
   which he is marvellously assisting.' *State Mysteries of the Jesuits* (1623),
   pp. 12–13.
25 St. Aldegundis (630–684) was the founder-abess of the Benedictine
   convent of Mauberge in Flanders and was famous for her patience
   during the ravages of cancer. St. Cunegunda (1224–1292) founded the
   convent at Sandeck and served the poor and the sick.
26 St. Marcella (d. 410) was a Roman matron who practised extreme
   asceticism after her husband's death. St. Polycarp, the Bishop of
   Smyrna, was martyred in 156.
27 St. Cecilia, a martyr of the second or third century, is the patroness of
   music and musicians. St. Ursula, according to legend, was the daughter
   of a Christian king in Britain.
28–29 As Bald points out (p. 138) leap year does not occur once every three
   years but 'is called bisextile because in the Julian Calendar the sixth day
   before the Kalends of March was counted twice in leap year'.

Into the nine and twentieth day of February;   30
There were no room else for me. See their love,
Their conscience too, to thrust me, a lame soldier,
Into leap-year. My wrath's up, and methinks
I could with the first syllable of my name
Blow up their colleges. Up, Error, wake,   35
Father of Supererogation, rise,
It is Ignatius calls thee, Loyola!
ERROR
    What have you done? Oh I could sleep in ignorance
Immortally, the slumber is so pleasing.
I saw the bravest setting for a game now   40
That ever my eye fixed on.
IGNATIUS   Game? What game?
ERROR
    The noblest game of all, a game at chess
Betwixt our side and the White House, the men set
In their just order ready to go to it.
IGNATIUS
    Were any of my sons placed for the game?   45
ERROR
    Yes, and a daughter too, a secular daughter
That plays the Black Queen's Pawn, he the Black Bishop's.
IGNATIUS
    If ever power could show a mastery in thee
Let it appear in this.
ERROR   'T is but a dream,
A vision you must think.   50

34–35 A pun on L. *ignis*, fire
48 *mastery* masterly operation

29–34 St. Ignatius's feast is actually on 31 July, so apparently Middleton's
    joke is based upon a misunderstanding. A soldier in early life, Loyola
    was wounded in the leg at the Siege of Pampeluna in 1521.
36 *Father of Supererogation*. A satirical allusion to the theological doctrine
    of works of supererogation, works forming a reserve fund of merit upon
    which sinners can draw. St. Ignatius, feeling slighted, calls for re-
    assurance concerning the meritorious works performed during his life.
40 Error's dream is a direct answer to Loyola's appeal. The results of St.
    Ignatius's meritorious works will be seen on the great chess board of
    world politics.
46 *a secular daughter*. That is, a member of the order founded several years
    before the date of the play by Mary Ward. The women of this order
    dressed on the model of the Jesuits and mingled freely with the world
    in order to aid the Jesuit cause.

IGNATIUS   I care not what
So I behold the children of my cunning
And see what rank they keep.

*Music. Enter severally in order of the game
the White and Black Houses*

ERROR   You have your wish,
Behold there's the full number of the game,
Kings and their Pawns, Queens, Bishops, Knights and
                                              Dukes.

IGNATIUS
Dukes? They're called Rooks by some.

ERROR   Corruptively!   55
Le Roc the word, *Custode de la Roche*,
The Keeper of the Forts, in whom both Kings
Repose much confidence, and for their trust-sake,
Courage and worth, do well deserve those titles.

IGNATIUS
The answer's high, I see my son and daughter.   60

ERROR
Those are two Pawns, the Black Queen's and Black
                                           Bishop's.

IGNATIUS
Pawns argue but poor spirits, and slight preferments,
Not worthy of the name of my disciples.
If I had stood so nigh, I would have cut

---

52 s.d. Q3. T omits

52 s.d. 'In order of the game' may be compared with 'in order set', Prologue, line 3, and with the even more explicit s.d. in A: 'Music—Enter
severally the White and Black Houses as they are set for the game'. If
the players at this entry really assumed 'the order of the game', the cast
must have numbered at least thirty-four. The White House would
presumably be on stage-right and the Black House, appropriately, on
the 'sinister side' (cf. *Ecclesiastes*, x, 2).

55–59 It is true that 'Rook' is derived from O.F. *roc* (rock or fortress),
but there is surely some point to this passage other than an etymological
one. The White Duke is, of course, Buckingham, who had received his
dukedom only a few months before the play was performed. This
passage thus appears to be a compliment to him; but if V.iii, 58–60,
118–123, and 211–212 are taken into account, one may notice that the
ensuing lines in the Induction, 62–68, are concerned with ruthless
social climbing. The whole question of the possible connection of
Buckingham with this play is one of its most puzzling aspects. See
Introduction, p. xv.

That Bishop's throat but I'd have had his place   65
And told the Queen a love-tale in her ear
Would make her best pulse dance. There's no elixir
Of brain or spirit amongst 'em.

ERROR
Why, would you have 'em play against themselves?
That's quite against the rule of game, Ignatius.   70

IGNATIUS
Push, I would rule myself, not observe rule.

ERROR
Why then you'd play a game all by yourself.

IGNATIUS
I would do anything to rule alone,
'Tis rare to have the world reigned in by one.

ERROR
See 'em anon, and mark 'em in their play,   75
Observe, as in a dance, they glide away.

IGNATIUS
Oh with what longings will this breast be tossed,
Until I see this great game won and lost.

---

71 *Push.* Brooke and Paradise print 'Pish' throughout, but 'Push' used as
an exclamation is one of Middleton's trade marks.

78 L, M, F, A, and Q3 have *exeunt* at the end of the Induction, but T, B,
Q1, and Q2 give no indication whether Ignatius and Error leave the
stage or remain, like Revenge and the Ghost of Andrea in *The Spanish
Tragedy.*

Act I, Scene i

Enter from the Black House THE BLACK QUEEN'S PAWN,
from the White House THE WHITE QUEEN'S PAWN

BLACK QUEEN'S PAWN
  I ne'er see that face but my pity rises,
When I behold so clear a masterpiece
Of heaven's art, wrought out of dust and ashes,
And at next thought to give her lost eternally,
In being not ours but the daughter of heresy,   5
My soul bleeds at mine eyes.
WHITE QUEEN'S PAWN   Where should truth speak
If not in such a sorrow? They're tears plainly,
Beshrew me if she weep not heartily.
What is my peace to her to take such pains in 't,
If I wander to loss and with broad eyes   10
Yet miss the path she can run blindfold in
Through often exercise, why should my oversight
Though in the best game that e'er Christian lost
Raise the least spring of pity in her eye?
'T is doubtless a great charity, and no virtue   15
Could win me sooner.

4 *give her* regard her as
10 *broad* wide open
12 *often* frequent

T has no scene divisions except at V.iii. The scene divisions here indicated are from L, M, A, and Q3 and thus were probably due entirely to Ralph Crane.
1 The chess game begins as the Black Queen's Pawn encounters her opposite number in the centre of the board. It should be remembered that either side could move first in seventeenth-century chess. The second move by Black occurs at line 31, as the Black Bishop's Pawn moves up to encounter the White Queen's Pawn. White's reply at line 196 is with his Bishop's Pawn, and the opening is clear: a Queen's Gambit Declined.
Edgar C. Morris's theory, in 'The Allegory in Middleton's *A Game at Chess*', *Englische Studien*, XXXVIII (1907), 39–52, has not won general acceptance. Morris argues that the Black Queen's Pawn is the Archduchess Isabella, the White Queen's Pawn is James's daughter Elizabeth, the Black Bishop's Pawn is Duke Maximilian of Bavaria, and the White Bishop's Pawn is James's son-in-law Frederick the Elector of the Palatinate. It seems most likely that Morris's theory is an over-elaboration of the two brief references to the Palatinate later in the play. Cf. I.i, 145–158.

BLACK QUEEN'S PAWN Blessed things prevail with 't!
  If ever goodness made a gracious promise
  It is in yonder look. What little pains
  Would build a fort for virtue to all memory
  In that sweet creature were the ground-work firmer. 20
WHITE QUEEN'S PAWN
    It has been all my glory to be firm
  In what I have professed.
BLACK QUEEN'S PAWN That is the enemy
  That steals your strength away, and fights against you,
  Disarms your soul e'en in the heat of battle.
  Your firmness that way makes you more infirm 25
  For the right Christian conflict. There I spied
  A zealous primative sparkle, but now flew
  From your devoted eye,
  Able to blow up all the heresies
  That ever sat in council with your spirit. 30

                Enter THE BLACK BISHOP'S PAWN:
                    a Jesuit

  And here comes he whose sanctimonious breath
  Can make that spark a flame. List to him, virgin,
  At whose first entrance princes will fall prostrate,
  Women are weaker vessels.
WHITE QUEEN'S PAWN By my penitence
  A comely presentation, and the habit, 35
  To admiration reverend.
BLACK QUEEN'S PAWN But the heart, the heart, lady;
  So meek, that as you see good Charity pictured still
  With young ones in her arms, so will he cherish
  All his young tractable sweet obedient daughters
  E'en in his bosom, in his own dear bosom. 40
  I am myself a secular Jesuit,
  As many ladies are of wealth and greatness;
  A second sort are Jesuits *in voto*,
  Giving their vow in to the Father General,
  That's the Black Bishop of our House, whose Pawn 45
  This gentleman now stands for, to receive
  The college habit at his holy pleasure.

27 *primative* revealing the depths of the soul
35 *presentation* address, appearance   43 *in voto* by vow, as novices
47 *habit* dress

37–38 Cf. *Faerie Queene*, I, x, 4, 16, 29–31.
41 See note on Induction, 46.

WHITE QUEEN'S PAWN
    But how are those *in voto* employed, lady,
    Till they receive the habit?
BLACK QUEEN'S PAWN   They're not idle;
    He finds 'em all true labourers in the work   50
    Of the universal monarchy, which he
    And his disciples principally aim at.
    Those are maintained in many courts and palaces,
    And are induced by noble personages
    Into great princes' services, and prove   55
    Some councillors of state, some secretaries,
    All serving in notes of intelligence,
    As parish clerks their mortuary bills,
    To the Father General; so are designs
    Oft times prevented, and important secrets   60
    Of states discovered, yet no author found
    But those suspected oft that are most sound.
    This mystery is too deep yet for your entrance
    And I offend to set your zeal so back.
    Checked by obedience with desire to hasten   65
    Your progress to perfection, I commit you
    To the great worker's hands, to whose grave worth
    I fit my reverence, as to you my wishes.
BLACK BISHOP'S PAWN
    [*Aside to* BLACK QUEEN'S PAWN] Dost find her supple?
BLACK QUEEN'S PAWN   There's a little passage made.
                         [*Exit*]
BLACK BISHOP'S PAWN
    Let me contemplate,   70
    With holy wonder season my access,

---

51 *universal monarchy* alleged Roman Catholic plan for world
    domination
54 *induced* introduced
57 *intelligence* information
60 *prevented* anticipated
61 *discovered* revealed, communicated
63 *for your entrance* for you to be introduced to
68 *reverence* obeisance

---

69 *There's . . . made.* In A;
                 There's a little passage:
    Women's poor arguments make but wimble-holes,
    The augur is the man's. *Exit*
The last two lines are deleted.

And by degrees approach the sanctuary
Of unmatched beauty set in grace and goodness.
Amongst the daughters of men I have not found
A more catholical aspect; that eye   75
Does promise single life and meek obedience;
Upon those lips, the sweet fresh buds of youth,
The holy dew of prayer lies like pearl
Dropped from the opening eyelids of the morn
Upon the bashful rose. How beauteously   80
A gentle fast not rigorously imposed
Would look upon that cheek, and how delightfully
The courteous physic of a tender penance
Whose utmost cruelty should not exceed
The first fear of a bride to beat down frailty   85
Would work to sound health your long festered judgment,
And make your merit, which through erring ignorance
Appears but spotted righteousness to me,
Far clearer than the innocence of infants.

WHITE QUEEN'S PAWN
　　To that good work I bow, and will become   90
Obedience' humblest daughter, since I find
Th' assistance of a sacred strength to aid me,
The labour is as easy to serve virtue
The right way, since 't is she I ever served
In my desire, though I transgressed in judgment.   95

BLACK BISHOP'S PAWN
　　That's easily absolved among the rest,
You shall not find the virtue that you serve now
A sharp and cruel mistress, her ear's open
To all your supplications, you may boldly
And safely let in the most secret sin   100
Into her knowledge, which like vanished man
Never returns into the world again;
Fate locks not up more trulier.

WHITE QUEEN'S PAWN　　　　　　　　To the guilty
That may appear some benefit.

BLACK BISHOP'S PAWN
　　Who is so innocent   105
That never stands in need on't, in some kind?

---

83 *courteous* mild

---

79 If Milton indeed took his 'opening eyelids of the morn' (*Lycidas*, 26)
　　from this line, Middleton may as well have been remembering *The Jew
　　of Malta*, II, 701: 'Now Phoebus ope the eyelids of the day.'

If every thought were blabbed that's so confessed
The very air we breathe would be unblessed.
[*Aside*] Now to the work indeed, which is to catch
Her inclination; that's the special use   110
We make of all our practice in all kingdoms,
For by disclosing their most secret frailties,
Things, which once ours, they must not hide from us,
That's the first article in the creed we teach 'em,
Finding to what point their blood most inclines,   115
Know best to apt them then to our designs.
[*To the* PAWN] Daughter! the sooner you disperse your
                                        errors,
The sooner you make haste to your recovery.
You must part with 'em: to be nice or modest
Toward this good action, is to imitate   120
The bashfulness of one conceals an ulcer,
For the uncomely parts the tumor vexes
Till't be past cure. Resolve you thus far, lady,
The privat'st thought that runs to hide itself
In the most secret corner of your heart now   125
Must be of my acquaintance, so familiarly
Never she-friend of your night-counsel nearer.

WHITE QUEEN'S PAWN
    I stand not much in fear of any action
Guilty of that black time, most noble holiness,
I must confess, as in a sacred temple   130
Thronged with an auditory, some come rather
To feed on human object, than to taste
Of angels' food;
So in the congregation of quick thoughts
Which are more infinite than such assemblies   135
I cannot with truth's safety speak for all.
Some have been wanderers, some fond, some sinful,
But those found ever but poor entertainment,
They'd small encouragement to come again.
The single life which strongly I profess now,   140
Heaven pardon me, I was about to part from.

BLACK BISHOP'S PAWN
    Then you have passed through love?

116 *apt* fit
117 *disperse* free yourself from
119 *nice* squeamish, fastidious
131 *auditory* congregation
134 *quick* living   137 *fond* foolish

WHITE QUEEN'S PAWN   But left no stain
  In all my passage, sir, no print of wrong
  For the most chaste maid that may trace my footsteps.
BLACK BISHOP'S PAWN
  How came you off so clear?
WHITE QUEEN'S PAWN   I was discharged   145
  By an inhuman accident, which modesty
  Forbids me to put any language to.
BLACK BISHOP'S PAWN
  How you forget yourself! All actions
  Clad in their proper language, though most sordid,
  My ear is bound by duty to let in   150
  And lock up everlastingly. Shall I help you?
  He was not found to answer his creation.
  A vestal virgin in a slip of prayer
  Could not deliver man's loss modestlier:
  'Twas the White Bishop's Pawn.
WHITE QUEEN'S PAWN   The same, blest sir.   155
BLACK BISHOP'S PAWN
  An heretic well pickled.
WHITE QUEEN'S PAWN   By base treachery
  And violence prepared by his competitor,
  The Black Knight's Pawn, whom I shall ever hate for't.
BLACK BISHOP'S PAWN
  'Twas of revenges the unmanliest way
  That ever rival took, a villainy   160
  That for your sake I'll ne'er absolve him of.
WHITE QUEEN'S PAWN
  I wish it not so heavy.
BLACK BISHOP'S PAWN   He must feel it;
  I never yet gave absolution
  To any crime of that unmanning nature.
  It seems then you refused him for defect;   165
  Therein you stand not pure from the desire

---

156 *well pickled* soured, a hopeless case

145–158 This curious passage offers the strongest support for Morris's
  explanation of the subplot. He argues that the Black Knight's Pawn's
  gelding of the White Bishop's Pawn represents the Duke of Bavaria's
  exclusion of the Elector Frederick from the throne of Bohemia, which
  prevented the union of the two strongest Protestant states in Germany.
  Bald, who rejects Morris's interpretation, suggests (pp. 13–14) that
  Middleton introduced this episode because he wished to satirize the
  Taxae Sacrae Poenitentiariae Apostolicae at IV.ii, 83-86.

That other women have in ends of marriage.
Pardon my boldness, if I sift your goodness
To the last grain.
WHITE QUEEN'S PAWN   I reverence your pains, sir,
And must acknowledge custom to enjoy   170
What other women challenge and possess
More ruled me than desire, for my desires
Dwell all in ignorance, and I'll never wish
To know that fond way may redeem them thence.
BLACK BISHOP'S PAWN
    [*Aside*] I never was so taken, beset doubly   175
Now with her judgment, what a strength it puts forth!
[*To the* PAWN] I bring work nearer to you, when you
                                                    have seen
A masterpiece of man, composed by heaven
For a great prince's favour, kingdom's love,
So exact, envy could not find a place   180
To stick a blot on person or on fame;
Have you not found ambition swell your wish then?
And desire steer your blood?
WHITE QUEEN'S PAWN   By virtue never.
I have only in the dignity of the creature
Admired the maker's glory.
BLACK BISHOP'S PAWN   [*Aside*] She's impregnable;   185
A second siege must not fall off so tamely.
She's one of those must be informed to know
A daughter's duty, which some take untaught.
Her modesty brings her behind-hand much;
My old means I must fly to, yes, 'tis it.   190
[*Gives a book*] Please you peruse this small tract of
                                                    obedience,
'Twill help you forward well.
WHITE QUEEN'S PAWN   Sir, that's a virtue
I ever thought on with especial reverence.
BLACK BISHOP'S PAWN
    You will conceive by that, my power, your duty.
WHITE QUEEN'S PAWN
    The knowledge will be precious of both, sir.   195

                Enter WHITE BISHOP'S PAWN

WHITE BISHOP'S PAWN
    [*Aside*] What makes yon troubler of all Christian waters

---

171 *challenge* claim as a right   177 *bring . . . you* question you more closely
181 *fame* reputation   196 *makes* does

So near that blessed spring? But that I know
Her goodness is the rock from whence it issues
Unmoveable as fate, 'twould more afflict me
Than all my suff'rings for her, which, so long   200
As she holds constant to the House she comes of,
The whiteness of the cause, the side, the quality,
Are sacrifices to her worth, and virtue,
And though confined, in my religious joys
I marry her and possess her.

BLACK BISHOP'S PAWN   Behold, lady,   205
The two inhuman enemies, the Black Knight's Pawn
And the White Bishop's, the gelder and the gelded.

Enter BLACK KNIGHT'S PAWN

WHITE QUEEN'S PAWN
There's my grief, my hate.
BLACK KNIGHT'S PAWN
[*Aside*] What, in the Jesuit's fingers? By this hand
I'll give my part now for a parrot's feather,   210
She never returns virtuous, 'tis impossible.
I'll undertake more wagers will be laid
Upon a usurer's return from hell
Than upon hers from him now; have I been guilty
Of such base malice that my very conscience   215
Shakes at the memory of, and when I look
To gather fruit find nothing but the savin tree
Too frequent in nuns' orchards, and there planted
By all conjecture to destroy fruit rather.
I will be resolved now. [*To the* WHITE QUEEN'S PAWN]
                                        Most noble virgin—   220
WHITE QUEEN'S PAWN
Ignoble villain! Dare that unhallowed tongue
Lay hold upon a sound so gracious?
What's nobleness to thee? Or virgin chastity?
They're not of thy acquaintance. Talk of violence
That shames creation, deeds would make night blush,   225
That's company for thee. Hast thou the impudence
To court me with a leprosy upon thee
Able to infect the walls of a great building?

204–205 though prevented from possessing her physically I am
        spiritually married to her
217 *savin tree* its leaves were used to cause abortions
220 *resolved* have my doubts resolved

BLACK BISHOP'S PAWN
   Son of offence, forbear, go set your evil
   Before your eyes. A penitential vesture   230
   Would better become you, some shirt of hair.
BLACK KNIGHT'S PAWN
   And you a three pound smock 'stead of an alb,
   An epicene chasuble. [*Aside*] This holy fellow
   Robs safe and close. I feel a sting that's worse too.—
   White Pawn! hast so much charity to accept   235
   A reconcilement, make thy own conditions
   For I begin to be extremely burdened.
WHITE BISHOP'S PAWN
   [*Aside*] No truth, or peace of that Black House protested
   Is to be trusted, but for hope of quittance
   And warned by diffidence I may entrap him soonest.   240
   [*To* BLACK KNIGHT'S PAWN] I admit conference.
BLACK KNIGHT'S PAWN   It is a nobleness
   That makes confusion cleave to all my merits.
   [*Exeunt* WHITE BISHOP'S PAWN *and* BLACK KNIGHT'S PAWN]
BLACK BISHOP'S PAWN
   That treatise will instruct you fully.

                    Enter BLACK KNIGHT

BLACK KNIGHT   [*Aside*] So, so,
   The business of the universal monarchy
   Goes forward well now, the great college pot   245
   That should be always boiling, with the fuel
   Of all intelligences possible
   Thorough the Christian kingdoms. Is this fellow
   Our prime incendiary, one of those
   That promised the White kingdom seven years since   250

233 *epicene chasuble* sleeveless vestment suitable for either sex
234 *close* secretly
239 *quittance* revenge
240 *diffidence* suspicion
247 *intelligences* news
248 *Thorough* through

---

243 s.d. The Black Knight was made up as the Count of Gondomar. 'They
   counter-feited his person to the life, with all his graces and faces, and
   had gotten (they say) a cast sute of his apparell for the purpose, and his
   Lytter, wherein, the world says, lackt nothing but a couple of asses to
   carrie yt, and Sir G. Peter, or Sir T. Mathew to beare him companie.'
   The Letters of John Chamberlain, ed. Norman Egbert McClure (Philadelphia, 1939), II, 577.

To our Black House? Put a new daughter to him,
The great work stands; he minds nor monarchy
Nor hierarchy (diviner principality).
I've bragged less,
But have done more than all the conclave on 'em,   255
Take their assistant fathers in all parts,
Ay, or their Father General in to boot.
And what I have done, I have done facetiously,
With pleasant subtlety and bewitching courtship,
Abused all my believers with delight;   260
They took a comfort to be cozened by me.
To many a soul, I have let in mortal poison
Whose cheeks have cracked with laughter to receive it;
I could so roll my pills in sugared syllables
And strew such kindly mirth o'er all my mischiefs,   265
They took their bane in way of recreation
As pleasure steals corruption into youth.
He spies me now, I must uphold his reverence,
Especially in public, though I know
Priapus, guardian of the cherry gardens,   270
Bacchus' and Venus' chit, is not more vicious.

BLACK BISHOP'S PAWN
    Blessings' accumulation keep with you, sir.

BLACK KNIGHT
    Honour's dissimulation be your due, sir.

WHITE QUEEN'S PAWN
    [*Aside*] How deep in duty his observance plunges,
His charge must needs be reverend.

BLACK BISHOP'S PAWN   I am confessor   275
    To this Black Knight too, you see devotion's fruitful,
Sh'as many sons and daughters.

BLACK KNIGHT   [*Aside*] I do this the more
    T' amaze our adversaries to behold
The reverence we give these guitonens,
And to beget a sound opinion   280

251–252 *Put . . . stands* confront him with a woman and he neglects
    the main business
252 *minds* is mindful of
252–254 lineation ed.
253 *hierarchy* the ecclesiastical hierarchy
260 *Abused* deceived
270 *Priapus* god of fruitfulness and procreative power, conventionally
    associated with lust
279 lazy *guitonen* beggars

Of holiness in them and zeal in us,
As also to invite the like obedience
In other pusills, by our meek example.—

                    [*Exit* WHITE QUEEN'S PAWN]

So, is your trifle vanished?

BLACK BISHOP'S PAWN
          Trifle call you her? 'Tis a good Pawn, sir;   285
Sure she's the second Pawn of the White House,
And to the opening of the game I hold her.

BLACK KNIGHT
          Ay, you
Hold well for that, I know your play of old.
If there were more Queen's Pawns you'd ply the game   290
A great deal harder (now, sir, we're in private).
But what for the main work, the great existence,
The hope monarchical?

BLACK BISHOP'S PAWN   It goes on in this.

BLACK KNIGHT
          In this? I cannot see't.

BLACK BISHOP'S PAWN   You may deny so
A dial's motion, 'cause you cannot see   295
The hand move, or a wind that rends the cedar.

BLACK KNIGHT
          Where stops the current of intelligence?
Your Father General, Bishop of the Black House,
Complains for want of work.

BLACK BISHOP'S PAWN   Here's from all parts
Sufficient to employ him: I received   300
A packet from the Assistant Fathers lately;
Look you, there's Anglica, this Gallica. [*Gives letters*]

283 *pusills* drabs 288–291 lineation ed.
292 *great existence* world empire
302 *Anglica* i.e., Anglica Provincia. The Jesuit missions were divided
    into provinces   *Gallica* French

---

287 *to . . . her.* He hopes to open up the game, and thus expose the King,
    by capturing the White Queen's Pawn.
292–296 A clear statement of the connection between the main and sub-
    sidiary plots of the play. The attempt on the individual human soul (the
    White Queen's Pawn) is shown to be a minor manifestation of the drive
    toward world dominion in the plot of the Spanish marriage and the
    attempt to convert Prince Charles.
298 This identifies one of the Black Bishops as the Father General of the
    Jesuit order. Apparently the other Bishop was intended to represent the
    Pope. See note on III.i, 25, 32–39.

BLACK KNIGHT
  Ay, marry, sir, there's some quick flesh in this.
BLACK BISHOP'S PAWN   [*Gives letter*] Germanica!
BLACK KNIGHT
  'Think they've sealed this with butter.
BLACK BISHOP'S PAWN   [*Gives letter*] Italica this!
BLACK KNIGHT
  They put their pens the Hebrew way methinks.   305
BLACK BISHOP'S PAWN
  Hispanica here! [*Gives letter*]
BLACK KNIGHT   Hispanica, blind work 'tis,
  The Jesuit has writ this with juice of lemons sure.
  It must be held close to the fire of purgatory
  Ere't can be read.
BLACK BISHOP'S PAWN You will not lose your jest, Knight,
  Though it wounded your own fame.

           Enter WHITE KING'S PAWN

BLACK KNIGHT   *Curanda pecunia.*   310
BLACK BISHOP'S PAWN
  Take heed, sir, we're entrapped. The White King's
                                         Pawn!
BLACK KNIGHT
  He's made our own man, half *in voto* yours,
  His heart's in the Black House, leave him to me.
                    [*Exit* BLACK BISHOP'S PAWN]
  Most of all friends endeared, preciously special!
WHITE KING'S PAWN
  You see my outside, but you know my heart, Knight,   315
  Great difference in the colour. There's some intelligence
  And, as more ripens, so your knowledge still

304 *'Think* I think L, M, Q3
306 *Hispanica* Spanish
307 *with . . . lemons* in invisible ink
310 *Curanda pecunia* money must be cared for
316 *intelligence* secret documents

---

305 An allusion to the difference between the Roman hand and the more
    common secretary hand.
310 *Curanda pecunia.* This phrase, which seems to have no necessary con-
    nection with the preceding lines, is evidently the Black Knight's
    exclamation on catching sight of the White King's Pawn. This may
    indicate that the White King's Pawn was immediately recognizable as
    the former Lord Treasurer, the Earl of Middlesex. For the com-
    posite origin of this character see Introduction, p. xiv.

Shall prove the richer; there shall nothing happen,
Believe it, to extenuate your cause
Or to oppress her friends, but I will strive   320
To cross it with my counsel, purse and power,
Keep all supplies back, both in means and men,
That may raise strength against you. We must part,
I dare not longer of this theme discuss,
The ear of state is quick and jealous.   325

BLACK KNIGHT
    Excellent estimation, thou art valued
Above the fleet of gold, that came short home.
                              [*Exit* WHITE KING'S PAWN]
Poor Jesuit-ridden soul, how art thou fooled
Out of thy faith, from thy allegiance drawn,
Which path soe'er thou tak'st thou'rt a lost Pawn.   330

Act II, Scene i

Enter WHITE QUEEN'S PAWN *with a book in her hand*

WHITE QUEEN'S PAWN
    And here again it is the daughter's duty
To obey her confessor's command in all things
Without exception or expostulation.
'T is the most general rule that e'er I read of,
Yet when I think how boundless virtue is,   5
Goodness and grace, 't is gently reconciled
And then it appears well to have the power
Of the dispenser as uncircumscribed.

Enter BLACK BISHOP'S PAWN

BLACK BISHOP'S PAWN
    [*Aside*] She's hard upon't: 't was the most modest key
That I could use to open my intents,   10

319 *extenuate* disparage, injure
321 *cross* defeat
323 *strength* ed. T omits
325 *jealous* T jealious L, F, A, Qq
327 *came short home* returned home after suffering losses, or failed to
    come home

318–323 *there . . . part.* Omitted in A. The lines in T and other manu-
    scripts which were added to the early version of the play are obviously
    an allusion to Middlesex's opposition in Council to Buckingham's desire
    for a war with Spain.

What little or no pains goes to some people.
Hah! a sealed note, whence this?
[*Reads*] 'To the Black Bishop's Pawn these.' How! to me?
Strange, who subscribes it? The Black King! What would
                                                          he?
[*Reads*] 'Pawn! sufficiently holy, but unmeasurably politic;   15
we had late intelligence from our most industrious servant
famous in all parts of Europe (our Knight of the Black
House), that you have at this instant in chase, the White
Queen's Pawn, and very likely by the carriage of your game
to entrap and take her. These are therefore to require you by   20
the burning affection I bear to the rape of devotion, that
speedily upon the surprisal of her, by all watchful advantage
you make some attempt upon the White Queen's person
whose fall or prostitution our lust most violently rages for.'
Sir, after my desire has took a julep   25
For its own inflammation, that yet scorches me,
I shall have cooler time to think of yours.
Sh'as passed the general rule, the large extent
Of our prescriptions for obedience,
And yet with what alacrity of soul   30
Her eye moves on the letters.
WHITE QUEEN'S PAWN   Holy sir,
Too long I have missed you; oh, your absence starves me!
Hasten for time's redemption, worthy sir,
Lay your commands as thick and fast upon me
As you can speak 'em; how I thirst to hear 'em!   35
Set me to work upon this spacious virtue
Which the poor span of life's too narrow for,

15 *politic* skilled in political manoeuvring
19 *carriage* play, conduct
21 *affection* inclination, desire
25 *julep* cooling drink
33 *hasten . . . redemption* hasten to make up for the lack

23 Morris (*op. cit.*, p. 42) interprets the White Queen as Queen Anne and
sees here an allusion to her conversion to the Roman Catholic faith.
However that may be, his further conclusion seems quite sound:
'. . . it must be kept in mind that the White Queen is not merely the
person of the late Queen Anne; it is the Queen standing for the Church
of England as the King represents the secular power of England, as
Gondomar represents the secular phases of the Jesuitical attempts to
convert England, and as the General of the Jesuits represents the
spiritual phases of the same movement.'

Boundless obedience,
The humblest yet the mightiest of all duties;
Well here set down a universal goodness.　　　　40

BLACK BISHOP'S PAWN
　　[*Aside*] By holiness of garment her safe innocence
Has frightened the full meaning from itself;
She's farder off from understanding now
The language of my intent than at first meeting.

WHITE QUEEN'S PAWN
　　For virtue's sake, good sir, command me something,　　45
Make trial of my duty in some small service
And as you find the faith of my obedience there,
Then trust it with a greater.

BLACK BISHOP'S PAWN　　　　You speak sweetly,
I do command you first then—

WHITE QUEEN'S PAWN　　　　With what joy
I do prepare my duty.

BLACK BISHOP'S PAWN　　To meet me　　　　50
And seal a kiss of love upon my lip.

WHITE QUEEN'S PAWN
　　Hah!

BLACK BISHOP'S PAWN　　At first disobedient, in so little too!
How shall I trust you with a greater then,
Which was your own request?

WHITE QUEEN'S PAWN　　　　Pray send not back
My innocence to wound me, be more courteous;　　55
I must confess much like an ignorant plantiff
Who presuming on the fair path of his meaning
Goes rashly on, till on a sudden brought
Into the wilderness of law, by words
Dropped unadvisedly, hurts his good cause　　　　60
And gives his adversary advantage by it.
Apply it you can best, sir, if my obedience
And your command can find no better way,
Fond men command, and wantons best obey.

BLACK BISHOP'S PAWN
　　If I can at that distance send you a blessing,　　65

38–40 lineation ed.　　43 *farder* further

64 *Fond . . . obey.* That is, what you have commanded is the sort of thing
　　commanded by foolish men and best obeyed by wantons.
65–67 Bald (p. 143) cites *The Friers Chronicle*, f. C IV: 'When any of the
　　Priests knauerie was discovered, there were excuses enough ready to
　　defend them; yes, when they were found kissing a woman; the answer
　　was, You must suppose he did it to print a blessing on her lips.'

Is it not nearer to you in mine arms?
It flies from these lips dealt abroad in parcels,
And I to honour thee above all daughters
Invite thee home to the House, where thou may'st surfeit
On that, which others miserably pine for,   70
A favour which the daughters of great potentates
Would look on envy's colour but to hear.
WHITE QUEEN'S PAWN
    Good men may err sometimes, you are mistaken sure.
    If this be virtue's path, 't is a most strange one,
    I never came this way before.
BLACK BISHOP'S PAWN   That's your ignorance,   75
    And therefore shall that idiot still conduct you
    That knows no way but one, nor ever seeks it.
    If there be twenty ways to some poor village
    'T is strange that virtue should be put to one;
    Your fear is wondrous faulty, cast it from you,   80
    'T will gather else in time a disobedience
    Too stubborn for my pardon.
WHITE QUEEN'S PAWN   Have I locked myself
    At unawares into sin's servitude
    With more desire of goodness? Is this the top
    Of all strict order? And the holiest   85
    Of all societies, the three-vowed people
    For poverty, obedience, chastity,
    The last the most forgot? When a virgin's ruined
    I see the great work of obedience
    Is better than half finished.
BLACK BISHOP'S PAWN   What a stranger   90
    Are you to duty grown, what distance keep you!
    Must I bid you come forward to a happiness
    Yourself should sue for? 'T was never so with me;
    I dare not let this stubbornness be known,
    'T would bring such fierce hate on you, yet presume not   95
    To make that courteous care a privilege
    For wilful disobedience; it turns then
    Into the blackness of a curse upon you.
    Come, come, be nearer.
WHITE QUEEN'S PAWN   Nearer?
BLACK BISHOP'S PAWN   Was that scorn?
    I would not have it prove so, for the hopes   100
    Of the grand monarchy; if it were like it

72 *on* of

Let it not dare to stir abroad again,
A stronger ill will cope with't.
WHITE QUEEN'S PAWN   Bless me, threatens me
And quite dismays the good strength that should help me.
I never was so doubtful of my safety.   105
BLACK BISHOP'S PAWN
'T was but my jealousy, forgive me, sweetness;
Yond is the house of meekness and no venom lives
Under that roof. Be nearer, why so fearful?
Nearer the altar the more safe and sacred.
WHITE QUEEN'S PAWN
But nearer to the offerer oft more wicked.   110
BLACK BISHOP'S PAWN
A plain and most insufferable contempt!
My glory I have lost upon this woman:
In freely offering that she should have kneeled
A year in vain for, my respect is darkened;
Give me my reverence again, thou hast robbed me of   115
In thy repulse, thou shalt not carry it hence.
WHITE QUEEN'S PAWN
Sir—
BLACK BISHOP'S PAWN
Thou art too great a winner to depart so
And I too deep a loser to give way to it.
WHITE QUEEN'S PAWN
Oh heaven!
BLACK BISHOP'S PAWN   Lay me down reputation   120
Before thou stir'st, thy nice virginity
Is recompence too little for my love,
'T is well if I accept of that for both.
Thy loss is but thine own, there's art to help thee
And fools to pass thee to; in my discovery   125
The whole Society suffers, and in that
The hope of absolute monarchy eclipsed.
Assurance thou canst make none for thy secrecy
But by thy honour's loss, that act must awe thee.
WHITE QUEEN'S PAWN
Oh my distressed condition!

103 *threatens* ed. threatnens T
104–105 lineation ed.
107 *Yond* T yours Q1, Q2
122 *love* T Dyce suggests loss
125 *in my discovery* if my act is revealed
126 *Society* Society of Jesus

BLACK BISHOP'S PAWN   Dost thou weep?   130
  If thou hadst any pity this necessity
  Would wring it from thee, I must else destroy thee;
  We must not trust the policy of Europe
  Upon a woman's tongue.
WHITE QUEEN'S PAWN   Then take my life, sir,
  And leave my honour for my guide to heaven.   135
BLACK BISHOP'S PAWN
  Take heed I take not both, which I have vowed
  Since if longer thou resist me—
WHITE QUEEN'S PAWN   Help, oh, help!
BLACK BISHOP'S PAWN
  Art thou so cruel for an honour's bubble
  To undo a whole fraternity, and disperse
  The secrets of most nations locked in us?   140
WHITE QUEEN'S PAWN
  For heaven and virtue's sake—
BLACK BISHOP'S PAWN   Must force confound—

                    A noise within

  Hah! What's that? Silence, if fair worth be in thee.
WHITE QUEEN'S PAWN
  I'll venture my escape upon all dangers now.
BLACK BISHOP'S PAWN
  Who comes to take me? Let me see that Pawn's face
  Or his proud tympanous master swelled with state wind   145
  Which being once pricked in the convocation house
  The corrupt air puffs out and he falls shrivelled.
WHITE QUEEN'S PAWN
  I will discover thee, arch-hypocrite,
  To all the kindreds of the earth.   [*Exit*]
BLACK BISHOP'S PAWN   Confusion!
  In that voice rings the alarm of my undoing.   150
  How! Which way 'scaped she from me?

                Enter BLACK QUEEN'S PAWN

BLACK QUEEN'S PAWN   Are you mad?
  Can lust infatuate a man so hopeful,

141 *confound* ed. confound noise T
143 *I'll . . . now* I'll try to escape whatever danger may threaten
145 *tympanous* empty
    state wind oratorical bombast
149 s.d. M, Q3 T omits
149–150 lineation ed.

No patience in your blood? The dog-star reigns sure;
Time and fair temper would have wrought her pliant.
I spied a Pawn of the White House walk near us   155
And made that noise a' purpose to give warning—
[*Aside*] For mine own turn, which end in all I work for.

BLACK BISHOP'S PAWN
        Methinks I stand over a powder-vault
And the match now a-kindling. What's to be done?

BLACK QUEEN'S PAWN
        Ask the Black Bishop's counsel; you're his Pawn,   160
'T is his own case, he will defend you mainly,
And happily here he comes with the Black Knight too.

        Enter BLACK BISHOP *and* BLACK KNIGHT

BLACK BISHOP
        Oh, y'ave made noble work for the White House yonder,
This act will fill the adversary's mouth
And blow the Lutheran's cheek, till't crack again.   165

BLACK KNIGHT
        This will advance the great monarchal business,
In all parts well, and help the agents forward.
What I in seven years laboured to accomplish
One minute sets back by some codpiece college still.

BLACK BISHOP'S PAWN
        I dwell not, sir, alone in this default,   170
The Black House yields me partners.

BLACK BISHOP   All more cautelous.

BLACK KNIGHT
        Qui caute, caste, that's my motto ever,
I have travelled with that word over most kingdoms
And lain safe with most nations, of a leaking bottom,
I have been as often tossed on Venus' seas   175
As trimmer fresher barks, when sounder vessels
Have lain at anchor, that is, kept the door.

153 *The . . . reigns* extreme heat has driven you mad
154–155 lineation ed.
157 *turn* purpose, advantage
161 *mainly* strongly
169 *codpiece* lascivious
170 *default* fault
171 *cautelous* careful, sly
172 *Qui . . . caste* he who acts prudently acts virtuously
173 *word* motto
174 *of . . . bottom* though in bad health (allusion to Gondomar's
        fistula)

BLACK BISHOP
 She has no witness then?
BLACK BISHOP'S PAWN   None, none.
BLACK KNIGHT   Gross, witness!
 When went a man of his Society
 To mischief with a witness?
BLACK BISHOP   I have done 't then.   180
 Away, upon the wings of speed take posthorse,
 Cast thirty leagues of earth behind thee suddenly,
 Leave letters antedated with our House
 Ten days at least from this.
BLACK KNIGHT   Bishop, I taste thee;
 Good strong episcopal counsel, take a bottle on 't, 185
 'T will serve thee all the journey.
BLACK BISHOP'S PAWN   But, good sir,
 How for my getting forth, unspied?
BLACK KNIGHT   There's check again.
BLACK QUEEN'S PAWN
 No, I'll help that!
BLACK KNIGHT   Well said, my bouncing Jesuitess.
BLACK QUEEN'S PAWN
 There lies a secret vault.
BLACK KNIGHT   Away, make haste then.
BLACK BISHOP'S PAWN
 Run for my cabinet of intelligences   190
 For fear they search the House. [*Exit* BLACK QUEEN'S PAWN]
     Good Bishop, burn 'em rather,
 I cannot stand to pick 'em now.
BLACK BISHOP   Be gone,
 The danger's all in you.

 [*Exit* BLACK BISHOP'S PAWN. *Enter* BLACK QUEEN'S PAWN
     with cabinet]

BLACK KNIGHT   Let me see, Queen's Pawn.
 How formally h'as packed up his intelligences,

180 *I . . . then* I see the solution
182 A, Qq. T omits
184 *taste thee* understand your meaning
192 *stand to pick* wait long enough to sort through
194 *formally* in order, neatly

---

183 *letters antedated.* Morris finds this passage difficult to accommodate to
 his interpretation of the allegory but suggests, unconvincingly, that the
 antedated letters are intended to represent Spinola's sealed orders from
 Spain before he marched on the Palatinate (*op. cit.*, p. 49).

H'as laid 'em all in tuckle-beds methinks, 195
And like court-harbingers has writ their names
In chalk upon their chambers. Anglica!
Oh, this is the English House, what news there, trow?
Hah! by this hand, most of these are bawdy epistles,
Time they were burnt indeed, whole bundles on 'em. 200
Here's from his daughter Blanche, and daughter Bridget,
For their safe sanctuary in the Whitefriars;
These from two tender Sisters of Compassion
In the bowels of Bloomsbury;
Three from the nunnery in Drury Lane. 205
A fire, a fire, good Jesuitess, a fire!
What have you there?

BLACK BISHOP   A note, sir, of state policy
And one exceeding safe one.

BLACK KNIGHT   Pray let's see it, sir—
[*Reads*] 'To sell away all the powder in a kingdom
To prevent blowing up.' That's safe, I'll able it. 210
Here's a facetious observation now,
And suits my humour better: he writes here
Some wives in England will commit adultery,
And then send to Rome for a bull for their husbands.

BLACK BISHOP
    Have they those shifts?

BLACK KNIGHT   Oh there's no female breathing 215
Sweeter and subtler; here, wench, take these papers,
Scorch me 'em soundly, burn 'em to French russet
And put 'em in again.

BLACK BISHOP   Why what's your mystery?

BLACK KNIGHT
    Oh sir, 't will mock the adversary strangely
If e'er the House be searched. 'T was done in Venice 220
Upon the Jesuitical expulse there,
When the inquisitors came all spectacled

195 *tuckle-beds* small beds fitting under larger
196 *court-harbingers* officers in charge of providing lodgings
198 *trow?* do you think?
202–205 *Whitefriars*, Bloomsbury and Drury Lane contained many
    Roman Catholics
210 *able* warrant, guarantee
221 *expulse* expulsion

220–225 In 1606 the Jesuits were expelled from Venice by the Signory for
    supporting the Pope after he had placed the Republic under an inter-
    dict.

To pick out syllables out of the dung of treason
As children pick out cherry-stones, yet found none
But what they made themselves with ends of letters.　　225
Do as I bid you, Pawn.

[Exit BLACK KNIGHT *and* BLACK BISHOP]

BLACK QUEEN'S PAWN　　　Fear not, in all,
I love roguery too well to let it fall.

Enter BLACK KNIGHT'S PAWN

How now! What news with you?

BLACK KNIGHT'S PAWN　　　　　The sting of conscience
Afflicts me so, for that inhuman violence
On the White Bishop's Pawn, it takes away　　　　230
My joy, my rest.

BLACK QUEEN'S PAWN　This 't is to make an eunuch;
You made a sport on 't then.

BLACK KNIGHT'S PAWN　　　Cease aggravation;
I come to be absolved for't, where's my confessor?
Why dost thou point to the ground?

BLACK QUEEN'S PAWN　　　　　'Cause he went that way.
Come, come help me in with this cabinet　　　　235
And after I have singed these papers throughly
I'll tell thee a strange story.

BLACK KNIGHT'S PAWN　　　If't be sad
'T is welcome.

BLACK QUEEN'S PAWN　'T is not troubled with much mirth, sir.

　　　　　　　　　　　　　　　　　　　Exeunt

Act II, Scene ii

Enter FAT BISHOP *with a* PAWN

FAT BISHOP
　　Pawn!

FAT BISHOP'S PAWN　I attend at your great holiness' service.

FAT BISHOP
　　For great I grant you, but for greatly holy,
　　There the soil alters, fat cathedral bodies

234 *that way* i.e., he has 'gone to ground'
236 *throughly* thoroughly

1　For the character of the Fat Bishop see Introduction, pp. xiv. Bald
　(pp. 7–10) gives a brief objective account of the activities of de Dominis.
　　A omits lines 1–99 of this scene. This early version shows that the
　satire on de Dominis was a late addition.
　　The original actor of the part of the Fat Bishop was probably William
　Rowley (see *T.L.S.*, 6 February, 1930).

Have very often but lean little souls
Much like the lady in the lobster's head,   5
A great deal of shell and garbage of all colours,
But the pure part that should take wings and mount
Is at last gasp, as if a man should gape
And from his huge bulk let forth a butterfly,
Like those big-bellied mountains which the poet   10
Delivers, that are brought abed with mouse-flesh.
Are my books printed, Pawn? My last invectives
Against the Black House?
FAT BISHOP'S PAWN   Ready for publication,
For I saw perfect books this morning, sir.
FAT BISHOP
    Fetch me a few which I will instantly   15
Distribute 'mongst the White House.
FAT BISHOP'S PAWN   With all speed, sir.
                                 [*Exit*]

FAT BISHOP
    'T is a most lordly life to rail at ease,
Sit, eat, and feed upon the fat of one kingdom,
And rail upon another with the juice on 't.
I have writ this book out of the strength and marrow   20
Of six and thirty dishes at a meal,
But most on 't out of cullis of cock-sparrows;
'T will stick and glue the faster to the adversary,
'T will slit the throat of their most calvish cause,
And yet I eat but little butcher's meat   25
In the conception.
Of all things I commend the White House best
For plenty and variety of victuals.
When I was one of the Black side professed

  5 *lady* actually a calcareous structure in the stomach of a lobster
11 *Delivers* describes
22 *cullis* a strong rich broth
25–27 lineation ed.

10–11 *Parturient montes, nascetur ridiculus mus.* Horace, *Ars Poetica*, 139.
12–13 While still an Archbishop in the Roman Church de Dominis had
    written *De Republica Ecclesiastica*, an attack on certain Roman Catholic
    doctrines; but he did not dare to publish his work until under the pro-
    tection of the English King. Other controversial works directed against
    Rome followed.
15–16 Middleton's satire on de Dominis's eagerness to circulate his writings
    appears to be quite just. See Bald, p. 143.
27–28 Cf. the satire on Spanish parsimony at V.iii, 6–55.

My flesh fell half a cubit, time to turn   30
When my own ribs revolted. But to say true
I have no preferment yet that's suitable
To the greatness of my person and my parts;
I grant I live at ease, for I am made
The master of the beds, the long-acre of beds,   35
But there's no marigolds that shuts and opens,
Flower-gentles, Venus-baths, apples of love,
Pinks, hyacinths, honeysuckles, daffadowndillies.
There was a time I had more such drabs than beds,
Now I've more beds than drabs;   40
Yet there's no eminent trader deals in wholesale
But she and I have clapped a bargain up,
Let in at Watergate, for which I have racked
My tenants' purse-strings that they have twanged again.

[*Enter* BLACK KNIGHT *and* BLACK BISHOP]

Yonder Black Knight, the fistula of Europe,   45
Whose disease once I undertook to cure
With a High Holborn halter—when he last
Vouchsafed to peep into my privileged lodgings
He saw good store of plate there, and rich hangings;
He knew I brought none to the White House with me.   50
I have not lost the use of my profession
Since I turned White House Bishop.

Enter his PAWN *with books*

BLACK KNIGHT   Look, more books yet.
Yond greasy turncoat gormandizing prelate
Does work our House more mischief by his scripts,
His fat and fulsome volumes,   55
Than the whole body of the adverse party.

44 s.d. F, Q1, Q2 T omits
47 *High Holborn* where executions took place

32–33 De Dominis was dissatisfied with the lucrative positions which he
    received from the English Church. His request for the Archbishopric
    of York was flatly refused by James.
34–35 De Dominis was appointed Master of the Hospital of the Savoy.
39–42 In the anonymous pamphlet *Newes from Rome, Spalato's Doome*
    (1624) de Dominis was accused of lechery.
43–44 De Dominis was apparently a very harsh landlord. See Fuller's
    Church History, Bk. X, 94.
47–50 Upon his arrival in England de Dominis received rich gifts from the
    King.

BLACK BISHOP
    Oh 't were a masterpiece of serpent subtlety
To fetch him a' this side again.

BLACK KNIGHT   And then damn him
Into the bag forever, or expose him
Against the adverse part which now he feeds upon,   60
And that would double damn him. My revenge
Has prompted me already, I'll confound him
A' both sides for the physic he provided
And the base surgeon he invented for me.
I'll tell you what a most uncatholic jest   65
He put upon me once, when my pain tortured me;
He told me he had found a present cure for me
Which I grew proud on, and observed him seriously.
What think you 't was? Being execution-day
He showed the hangman to me at a window,   70
The common hangman.

BLACK BISHOP   Oh insufferable!

BLACK KNIGHT
    I'll make him the balloon-ball of the churches
And both the sides shall toss him; he looks like one,
A thing swelled up with mingled drink and urine,
And will bound well from one side to another!   75
Come, you shall write, our second Bishop absent
(Which has yet no employment in the game,
Perhaps nor ever shall, it may be won
Without his motion, it rests most in ours),
He shall be flattered with *sede vacante*;   80
Make him believe he comes into his place
And that will fetch him with a vengeance to us,
For I know powder is not more ambitious
When the match meets it, than his mind for mounting;
As covetous, and lecherous—

---

60 *part* T party Q1, Q2
68 *proud on* interested in
72 *baloon-ball* a large inflated ball struck back and forth with sticks
80 *sede vacante* an available position in the Church

58–64 Gondomar was popularly supposed to have been instrumental in de
    Dominis's re-conversion to Rome. See *Newes from Rome . . .*, Chap.
    IV, pp. 22–24.
76–79 The second Black Bishop is apparently the Pope. See note on III i,
    25, 32–39.

BLACK BISHOP No more now, sir, 85
  Both the sides fill.

Enter both Houses

WHITE KING This has been looked for long.
FAT BISHOP
  The stronger sting it shoots into the blood
  Of the Black adversary; I am ashamed now
  I was theirs ever, what a lump was I
  When I was led in ignorance and blindness; 90
  I must confess,
  I have all my life-time played the fool till now.
BLACK KNIGHT
  And now he plays two parts, the fool and knave.
FAT BISHOP
  There is my recantation in the last leaf
  Writ like a Ciceronian in pure Latin. 95
WHITE BISHOP
  Pure honesty, the plainer Latin serves then.
BLACK KNIGHT
  Plague of those pestilent pamphlets, those are they
  That wound our cause to the heart.
BLACK BISHOP Here comes more anger.
BLACK KNIGHT
  But we come well provided for this storm.

Enter WHITE QUEEN'S PAWN

WHITE QUEEN
  Is this my Pawn? She that should guard our person, 100
  Or some pale figure of dejection
  Her shape usurping? Sorrow and affrightment
  Has prevailed strangely with her.
WHITE QUEEN'S PAWN King of integrity!
  Queen of the same, and all the House professors
  Of noble candour, uncorrupted justice 105
  And truth of heart: through my alone discovery—
  My life and honour wondrously preserved—
  I bring into your knowledge with my sufferings,

91–93 lineation ed.
106 *alone* single

---

86 *This . . . long.* Referring to the full public proof of the conversion of the
  Fat Bishop as manifested in his works. Probably the Fat Bishop presents a book to the White King at this line.

Fearful affrightments, and heart-killing terrors
The great incendiary of Christendom, 110
The absolut'st abuser of true sanctity,
Fair peace and holy order can be found
In any part of the universal globe,
Who making meek devotion keep the door—
His lips being full of holy zeal at first— 115
Would have committed a foul rape upon me.

WHITE QUEEN
    Hah!

WHITE KING
    A rape! that's foul indeed, the very sound
To our ear fouler than the offence itself
To some kings of the earth.

WHITE QUEEN'S PAWN   Sir, to proceed, 120
Gladly I offered life to preserve honour
Which would not be accepted without both,
The chief of his ill aim being at my honour,
Till heaven was pleased by some unlooked for accident
To give me courage to redeem myself. 125

WHITE KING
    When we find desperate sins in ill men's companies
We place a charitable sorrow there
But custom and their leprous inclination
Quits us of wonder, for our expectation
Is answered in their lives; but to find sin, 130
Ay, and a masterpiece of darkness, sheltered
Under a robe of sanctity, is able
To draw all wonder to that monster only
And leave created monsters unadmired.
The pride of him that took first fall for pride 135
Is to be angel-shaped, and imitate
The form from whence he fell; but this offender,
Far baser than sin's master, fixed by vow
To holy order, which is angels' method,
Takes pride to use that shape to be a devil. 140
It grieves me that my knowledge must be tainted
With his infested name;
Oh rather with thy finger point him out.

112 *can* that can   114 *keep the door* act as pander
126–127 lineation ed.   142 *infested* T infected Q3

118–120 Probably an allusion to the seizure of the Palatinate. This is one of
    the principal supports of Morris's explanation of the subplot.

WHITE QUEEN'S PAWN
 The place which he should fill is void, my lord,
His guilt has seized him; the Black Bishop's Pawn. 145
BLACK BISHOP
 Hah! mine? My Pawn? The glory of his order;
The prime and president zealot of the earth,
Impudent Pawn! For thy sake at this minute
Modesty suffers, all that's virtuous blushes,
And truth's self like the sun vext with a mist 150
Looks red with anger.
WHITE BISHOP Be not you drunk with rage too.
BLACK BISHOP
 Sober sincerity! Nor you a cup
Spiced with hypocrisy.
WHITE KNIGHT You name there, Bishop,
But your own Christmas-bowl, your morning's draught
Next your episcopal heart all the twelve days, 155
Which smack you cannot leave all the year following.
BLACK KNIGHT
 A shrewd retort!
H'as made our Bishop smell of burning too;
Would I stood farder off were't no impeachment
To my honour or the game, would they'd play faster. 160
White Knight! there is acknowledged from our House
A reverence to you, and a respect
To that loved Duke stands next you; with the favour
Of the White King, and the aforenamed respected,
I combat with this cause. If with all speed— 165
Waste not one syllable, unfortunate Pawn,
Of what I speak—thou dost not plead distraction,
A plea which will but faintly take thee off neither
From this leviathan-scandal that lies rolling
Upon the crystal waters of devotion; 170
Or, what may quit thee more, though enough nothing,

144 *lord* Q3 *L* T
147 *president* chief
151 *with* Q3 T omits
171 *quit* acquit
 enough nothing not sufficiently

___

159 *Would . . . off.* The Knight's place in the initial position is, of course,
 immediately next to the Bishop's,
160 *would . . . faster.* A remark typical of the Black Knight who cannot
 endure the stately formality of the preceding speeches and now makes
 his own devious move.

Fall down and foam, and by that pang discover
The vexing spirit of falsehood strong within thee;
Make thyself ready for perdition,
There's no remove in all the game to 'scape it;   175
This Pawn, or this, the Bishop or myself,
Will take thee in the end, play how thou canst.

WHITE QUEEN'S PAWN
    Spite of sin's glorious ostentation,
And all loud threats, those thundercracks of pride
Ush'ring a storm of malice, House of Impudence,   180
Craft and equivocation, my true cause
Shall keep the path it treads in.

BLACK KNIGHT   I play thus then:
Now in the hearing of this high assembly
Bring forth the time of this attempt's conception.

WHITE QUEEN'S PAWN
    Conception! Oh how tenderly you handle it.   185

WHITE BISHOP
    It seems, Black Knight, you are afraid to touch it.

BLACK KNIGHT
    Well, its eruption: will you have it so then?
Or you, White Bishop, for her? The uncleaner,
Vile and more impious that you urge the strain to,
The greater will her shame's heap show i' th'end   190
And the wronged meek man's glory. The time, Pawn!

WHITE QUEEN'S PAWN
    Yesterday's cursed evening.

BLACK KNIGHT   Oh the treasure
Of my revenge I cannot spend all on thee,
Ruin enough to spare for all thy kindred too.
For honour's sake call in more slanderers: 195
I have such plentiful confusion,
I know not how to waste it. I'll be nobler yet
And put her to her own house. King of meekness,
Take the cause to thee, for our hands too heavy,
Our proofs will fall upon her like a tower   200
And grind her bones to powder.

175 *remove* move
189 *strain* recital
197 *waste* expend

---

181 A reference to the Jesuit doctrine of 'equivocation'. See G. B. Harrison,
    Last Elizabethan Journal (1933), pp. 111, 218–219.

WHITE QUEEN'S PAWN   What new engine
  Has the devil raised in him now?
BLACK KNIGHT   Is it he?
  And that the time? Stand firm now to your scandal,
  Pray do not shift your slander.
WHITE QUEEN'S PAWN   Shift your treacheries,
  They've worn one suit too long.
BLACK KNIGHT   That holy man,   205
  So wrongfully accused by this lost Pawn,
  Has not been seen these ten days in these parts.
WHITE KNIGHT
  How!
BLACK KNIGHT
  Nay at this instant thirty leagues from hence.
WHITE QUEEN'S PAWN
  Fathomless falsehood! Will it 'scape unblasted?   210
WHITE KING
  Can you make this appear?
BLACK KNIGHT   Light is not clearer;
  By his own letters, most impartial monarch!
WHITE KING'S PAWN
  How wrongfully may sacred virtue suffer, sir.
BLACK KNIGHT
  [*Aside*] Bishop, we have a treasure of that false heart.
WHITE KING
  Step forth and reach those proofs.
                    [*Exit a* BLACK PAWN *who returns with papers*]
WHITE QUEEN'S PAWN   Amazement covers me!   215
  Can I be so forsaken of a cause
  So strong in truth and equity? Will virtue
  Send me no aid in this hard time of friendship?
BLACK KNIGHT
  [*Aside*] There's an infallible staff and a red hat
  Reserved for you.
WHITE KING'S PAWN   Oh sir endeared!
BLACK KNIGHT   [*Aside*] A staff   220
  That will not easily break, you may trust to it;
  And such a one had your corruption need of.
  There's a state-fig for you now.

201 *engine* device
219 *red hat* cardinal's hat   223 *state-fig* diplomatic insult

219 *red hat*. This is a suggestion which seems very odd in connection with
  Middlesex and more appropriate to Sir Toby Matthew.

WHITE KING   Behold all,
How they cohere in one. I always held
A charity so good to holiness professed;   225
I ever believed rather
The accuser false than the professor vicious.
BLACK KNIGHT
A charity like all your virtues else,
Gracious and glorious.
WHITE KING   Where settles the offence,
Let the fault's punishment be derived from thence: 230
We leave her to your censure.
BLACK KNIGHT   Most just majesty!
    [*Exeunt* WHITE KING, QUEEN, BISHOP, KING'S PAWN,
            FAT BISHOP, FAT BISHOP'S PAWN]
WHITE QUEEN'S PAWN
Calamity of virtue! My Queen leave me too!
Am I cast off as the olive casts her flower?
Poor harmless innocence, art thou left a prey
To the devourer?
WHITE KNIGHT   No thou art not lost;   235
Let 'em put on their bloodiest resolutions
If the fair policy I aim at prospers.
Thy counsel, noble Duke!
WHITE DUKE   For that work cheerfully.
WHITE KNIGHT
A man for speed now!
WHITE BISHOP'S PAWN   Let it be my honour, sir,
Make me that flight that owes her my life's service.   240
        Exeunt WHITE KNIGHT, DUKE, *and* BISHOP'S PAWN
BLACK KNIGHT
Was not this brought about well for our honours?
BLACK BISHOP
Push, that Galician sconce can work out wonders.

224 *they . . . one* how the proofs hang together
224–227 lineation ed.
232 *Queen* A, Q3 frend T
240 *flight* a type of arrow made for long shots
242 *Galician sconce* Spanish brain

---

231 Morris (*op. cit.*, p. 48) interprets this action as James's refusal to allow
    Elizabeth to visit England and to the terms of the treaty of peace which
    allowed Ferdinand and Spain to dictate the submission of Frederick.
235–240 Charles and Buckingham were very much in favour of a strong line
    in Germany after the failure of the Spanish marriage negotiations.

BLACK KNIGHT
　　Let's use her as upon the like discovery
　　A maid was used at Venice, everyone
　　Be ready with a penance. Begin, majesty.   245
　　Vessel of foolish scandal! Take thy freight:
　　Had there been in that cabinet of niceness
　　Half the virginity of the earth locked up
　　And all swept at one cast by the dexterity
　　Of a Jesuitical gamester, 't had not valued   250
　　The least part of that general worth thou hast tainted.
BLACK KING
　　First I enjoin thee to a three days' fast for 't.
BLACK QUEEN
　　You're too penurious, sir, I'll make it four.
BLACK BISHOP
　　And I to a twelve hours' kneeling at one time.
BLACK KNIGHT
　　And in a room filled all with Aretine's pictures,   255
　　More than the twice twelve labours of luxury;
　　Thou shalt not see so much as the chaste pommel
　　Of Lucrece' dagger peeping; nay, I'll punish thee
　　For a discoverer, I'll torment thy modesty.
BLACK DUKE
　　After that four days' fast to the Inquisition-house,   260
　　Strengthened with bread and water for worse penance.
BLACK KNIGHT
　　Why, well said, Duke of our House, nobly aggravated!
WHITE QUEEN'S PAWN
　　Virtue, to show her influence more strong,
　　Fits me with patience mightier than my wrong.   *Exeunt*

Act III, Scene i

Enter FAT BISHOP

FAT BISHOP
　　I know my pen draws blood of the Black House,
　　There's never a book I write but their cause bleeds;
　　It has lost many an ounce of reputation

---

256 *luxury* lust   259 *discoverer* revealer of a secret

255–256 A reference to Giulio Romano's illustrations to a series of obscene
　　poems by Pietro Aretino.
　1–79 Omitted in A. Cf. note on II.ii, 1. For the probable source of this
　　passage see note on II.ii, 58–64.

Since I came of this side, I strike deep in
And leave the orifex gushing where I come;   5
But where's my advancement all this while I ha' gaped
                                                    for 't?
I'd have some round preferment, corpulent dignity
That bears some breadth and compass in the gift on 't;
I am persuaded that this flesh would fill
The biggest chair ecclesiastical   10
If it were put to trial.
To be made master of an hospital
Is but a kind of diseased bed-rid honour,
Or dean of the poor alms knights that wear badges.
There's but two lazy beggarly preferments   15
In the White Kingdom, and I have got 'em both;
My spirit does begin to be crop-sick
For want of other titles.

                    Enter BLACK KNIGHT

BLACK KNIGHT   [*Aside*] Oh here walks
His fulsome holiness; now for the master-trick
T' undo him everlastingly that's put home   20
And make him hang in hell most seriously
That jested with a halter upon me.
FAT BISHOP
[*Aside*] The Black Knight! I must look to my play then.
BLACK KNIGHT
I bring fair greetings to your reverend virtues
From Cardinal Paulus, your most princely kinsman.   25
                                    [*Gives a letter*]
FAT BISHOP
Our princely kinsman, say'st thou? We accept 'em.
Pray keep your side and distance, I am chary
Of my episcopal person;

5 *orifex* wound
14 *poor alms knights* the Poor Knights of Windsor

---

14 A few months after his appointment as Master of the Savoy de Dominis
was granted the Deanery of Windsor. Dyce quotes Hackett's *Life of
Archbishop Williams* (1693) to the effect that these two preferments
together were worth £800 per annum.
25, 32–39 Paul V died in 1621 and was succeeded in 'the Papal dignity' by
Gregory XV (Cardinal Paulus) who had been de Dominis's friend years
before. We seem to have here the identity of the other Black Bishop to
whom the Black Knight referred earlier. See note on II.ii, 76–79.

I know the Knight's walk in this game too well,
He may skip over me, and where am I then?   30
BLACK KNIGHT
  [*Aside*] There where thou shalt be shortly if art fail not.
FAT BISHOP
  [*Reads*] 'Right reverend and noble'—meaning ourself—
'our true kinsman in blood, but alienated in affection, your
unkind disobedience to the mother cause proves at this time
the only cause of your ill fortune. My present remove by   35
election to the papal dignity had now auspiciously settled you
in my *sede vacante*'—hah! had it so—'which by my next
remove by death might have proved your step to
supremacy.'
How! All my body's blood mounts to my face   40
To look upon this letter.
BLACK KNIGHT   The pill works with him.
FAT BISHOP
  [*Reads*] 'Think on it seriously, it is not yet too late
through the submiss acknowledgement of your disobedience
to be lovingly received into the brotherly bosom of the
conclave.'   45
[*Aside*] This was the chair of ease I ever aimed at.
I'll make a bonfire of my books immediately,
All that are left against that side I'll sacrifice,
Pack up my plate and goods and steal away
By night at water-gate; it is but penning   50
Another recantation, and inventing
Two or three bitter books against the White House
And then I'm in a' t'other side again
As firm as e'er I was, as fat and flourishing.—
Black Knight! expect a wonder ere 't be long;   55
You shall see me one of the Black House shortly.

29 *walk* move
32 speech heading omitted in T
35 *remove* removal
37 *by my* T at my Qq
42 speech heading omitted in T
43 *submiss* submissive

30–31 The Knight's 'wriggling move', one square forward and one diagon-
    ally, is notoriously deceptive, and the Knight is the only chessman
    which can leap over a square occupied by another piece.
51 This may refer specifically to *Marcus Antonius de Dominis, Archiepisc.*
    Spalaten, sui reditus ex Anglia consilium exponit, Romae, Rome, 1623.
    The authenticity of this 'recantation' has been questioned.

BLACK KNIGHT
Your holiness is merry with the messenger,
Too happy to be true, you speak what should be,
If natural compunction touched you truly.
Oh y'ave drawn blood, life-blood, the blood of honour,   60
From your most dear, your primitive mother's heart,
Your sharp invectives have been points of spears
In her sweet tender sides; the unkind wounds
Which a son gives, a son of reverence specially,
They rankle ten times more than the adversary's.   65
I tell you, sir, your reverend revolt
Did give the fearfulest blow to adoration
Our cause e'er felt, it shook the very statues,
The urns and ashes of the sainted sleepers.

FAT BISHOP
Forbear, or I shall melt in the place I stand   70
And let forth a fat bishop in sad syrup;
Suffices, I am yours when they least dream on 't.
Ambition's fodder, power and riches draws me,
When I smell honour that's the lock of hay
That leads me through the world's field every way.   *Exit*   75

BLACK KNIGHT
Here's a sweet paunch to propagate belief on,
Like the foundation of a chapel laid
Upon a quagmire. I may number him now
Amongst my inferior policies and not shame 'em;
But let me a little solace my designs   80
With the remembrance of some brave ones past
To cherish the futurity of project
Whose motion must be restless, till that great work
Called the possession of the world be ours.
Was it not I proclaimed a precious safeguard   85
From the White Kingdom to secure our coasts
'Gainst the infidel pirate, under pretext
Of more necessitous expedition?
Who made the jails fly open, without miracle,
And let the locusts out, those dangerous flies   90

---

61 *primitive* original

85–88 With great diplomatic skill Gondomar in 1620 persuaded the
    English to fight the Turks who had been proving very annoying to
    Spain.
89–99 Gondomar persuaded James to release the imprisoned priests and
    Jesuits during the negotiations for the Spanish marriage.

Whose property is to burn corn with touching?
The heretic granaries feel it to this minute,
And now they have got amongst the country-crops
They stick so fast to the converted ears
The loudest tempest that authority rouses   95
Will hardly shake 'em off; they have their dens
In ladies' couches, there's safe groves and fens;
Nay, were they followed and found out by th' scent,
Palm-oil will make a pursuivant relent.
Whose policy was 't to put a silenced muzzle   100
On all the barking tongue-men of the time,
Made pictures that were dumb enough before
Poor sufferers in that politic restraint?
My light spleen skips and shakes my ribs to think on 't.
Whilst our drifts walked uncensured but in thought,   105
A whistle or a whisper would be questioned,
In the most fortunate angle of the world.
The court has held the city by the horns
Whilst I have milked her; I have had good sops too
From country ladies for their liberties,   110
From some, for their most vainly hoped preferments,
High offices in the air. I should not live
But for this *mel aerium*, this mirth-manna.
My Pawn! How now! The news!

Enter his PAWN

BLACK KNIGHT'S PAWN
    Expect none very pleasing   115
That comes, sir, of my bringing, I'm for sad things.
BLACK KNIGHT
    Thy conscience is too tender-hoofed o' late,
    Every nail pricks it.

 99 *Palm-oil* bribery
    pursuivant officer who enforced ecclesiastical laws
104 *spleen* regarded as the cause of violent mirth
104–106 lineation ed.
105 *drifts* intentions, schemes
110–122 lineation ed.
113 *mel aerium* airy honey

100–101 While the negotiations for the Spanish marriage were in progress,
    preachers, many of whom opposed it, were forbidden to discuss affairs
    of state.
102–103 'The reference here is to an engraving by the Rev. Samuel Ward, of
    Ipswich, called *1588 Deo Trin-uni Britanniae*, which was suppressed'
    (Bald).

BLACK KNIGHT'S PAWN   This may prick yours too
   If there be any quick flesh in a yard on 't.
BLACK KNIGHT
      Mine?   120
   Mischief must find a deeper nail and a driver
   Beyond the strength of any Machiavel
   The politic kingdoms fatten, to reach mine.
   Prithee, compunction needle-pricked, a little
   Unbind this sore wound.
BLACK KNIGHT'S PAWN   Sir, your plot's discovered. 125
BLACK KNIGHT
      Which of the twenty thousand and nine hundred
   Four score and five, canst tell?
BLACK KNIGHT'S PAWN   Bless us, so many?
   How do poor countrymen have but one plot
   To keep a cow on, yet in law for that?
   You cannot know 'em all sure by their names, sir.   130
BLACK KNIGHT
      Yes, were their number trebled. Thou hast seen
   A globe stands on the table in my closet?
BLACK KNIGHT'S PAWN
      A thing, sir, full of countries and hard words?
BLACK KNIGHT
      True, with lines drawn some tropical, some oblique.
BLACK KNIGHT'S PAWN
      I can scarce read, I was brought up in blindness. 135
BLACK KNIGHT
      Just such a thing, if e'er my skull be opened,
   Will my brains look like.
BLACK KNIGHT'S PAWN   Like a globe of countries.
BLACK KNIGHT
      Ay, and some master-politician
   That has sharp state-eyes will go near to pick out
   The plots, and every climate where they fastened;   140
   'T will puzzle 'em too.
BLACK KNIGHT'S PAWN   I'm of your mind for that, sir.
BLACK KNIGHT
      They'll find 'em to fall thick upon some countries;
   They'd need to use spectacles. But I turn to you now,
   What plot is that discovered?
BLACK KNIGHT'S PAWN   Your last brat, sir,
   Begot 'twixt the Black Bishop and yourself,   145
   Your ante-dated letters 'bout the Jesuit.

BLACK KNIGHT
    Discovered? How?
BLACK KNIGHT'S PAWN   The White Knight's policy
    Has outstripped yours, it seems,
    Joined with the assistant counsel of his Duke.
    The Bishop's White Pawn undertook the journey   150
    Who as they say discharged it like a flight,
    I made him for the business fit and light.
BLACK KNIGHT
    'T is but a bawdy Pawn out of the way a little,
    Enow of them in all parts.

         Enter BLACK BISHOP *and both the Houses*

BLACK BISHOP   You have heard all then?
BLACK KNIGHT
    The wonder's past with me, but some shall down for 't.   155
WHITE KNIGHT
    Set free that virtuous Pawn from all her wrongs,
    Let her be brought with honour to the face
    Of her malicious adversary.
                       [Exit a WHITE PAWN]
BLACK KNIGHT   Good!
WHITE KING
    Noble chaste Knight, a title of that candour
    The greatest prince on earth without impeachment   160
    May have the dignity of his worth comprised in,
    This fair delivering act virtue will register
    In that white book of the defence of virgins
    Where the clear fame of all preserving knights
    Are to eternal memory consecrated;   165
    And we embrace as partner of that honour
    This worthy Duke, the counsel of the act,
    Whom we shall ever place in our respect.
WHITE DUKE
    Most blest of kings! throned in all royal graces,
    Every good deed sends back its own reward   170
    Into the bosom of the enterpriser;
    But you to express yourself as well to be
    King of munificence as integrity
    Adds glory to the gift.
WHITE KING   Thy deserts claim it,
    Zeal and fidelity.—Appear thou beauty   175

171 *enterpriser* performer
172 *you* for you

Of truth and innocence, best ornament
Of patience, thou that mak'st thy sufferings glorious.

[*Enter* WHITE PAWN *with* WHITE QUEEN'S PAWN]

BLACK KNIGHT
    [*Aside*] I'll take no knowledge on 't.—What makes she
                                         here?
How dares yon Pawn unpenanced, with a cheek
Fresh as her falsehood yet, where castigation   180
Has left no pale print of her visiting anguish,
Appear in the assembly? [*Aside*] Let me alone;
Sin must be bold, that's all the grace 't is born to.

WHITE KNIGHT
    What's this?

WHITE KING   I'm wonder-struck!

WHITE QUEEN'S PAWN   Assist me, goodness,
    I shall to prison again.

BLACK KNIGHT   [*Aside*] At least I have mazed 'em,   185
Shattered their admiration of her innocence
As the fired ships put in severed the fleet
In eighty-eight. I'll on with it; impudence
Is mischief's patrimony.—Is this justice?
Is injured reverence no sharplier righted?   190
I ever held that majesty impartial
That like most equal heavens looks on the manners,
Not on the shapes they shroud in.

WHITE KING   That Black Knight
Will never take an answer, 't is a victory
To make him understand he does amiss   195
When he knows in his own clear understanding
That he does nothing else. Show him the testimony
Confirmed by good men, how that foul attempter
Got but this morning to the place, from whence
He dated his forged lines for ten days past.   200

BLACK KNIGHT
    Why may not that corruption sleep in this

178 *makes* does
184 *What's this?* Q3 whats tis T
185 *mazed* confused
192 *equal* just
192–193 *looks . . . in* judges fact rather than appearances
201–203 May not the evil which you rashly see in our story actually
    be in this other that contradicts it

187 *fired ships* were used by the English against the Armada at Calais.

By some connivance, as you have waked in ours
By too rash confidence?
WHITE DUKE   I'll undertake
That Knight shall teach the devil how to lie.
WHITE KNIGHT
    If sin were half as wise as impudent   205
    She'd ne'er seek farder for an advocate.

Enter BLACK QUEEN'S PAWN

BLACK QUEEN'S PAWN
    [*Aside*] Now to act treachery with an angel's tongue;
    Since all's come out, I'll bring him strangely in again.—
    Where is this injured chastity, this goodness
    Whose worth no transitory piece can value,   210
    This rock of constant and invincible virtue
    That made sin's tempest weary of his fury?
BLACK QUEEN
    What, is my Pawn distracted?
BLACK KNIGHT   I think rather
    There is some notable masterprize of roguery
    This drum strikes up for.
BLACK QUEEN'S PAWN   Let me fall with reverence   215
    Before this blessed altar.
BLACK QUEEN   This is madness.
BLACK KNIGHT
    Well, mark the end; I stand for roguery still,
    I will not change my side.
BLACK QUEEN'S PAWN   I shall be taxed, I know;
    I care not what the Black House thinks of me.
BLACK QUEEN
    What say you now?
BLACK KNIGHT   I will not be unlaid yet.   220
BLACK QUEEN'S PAWN
    How any censure flies, I honour sanctity,
    That is my object, I intend no other;
    I saw this glorious and most valiant virtue
    Fight the most noblest combat with the devil.

208 *bring . . . again* restore things miraculously to their original
    condition
208–209 lineation ed.
210 *value* equal in price
218 *taxed* held accountable
220 *unlaid* disturbed
221 *How . . . flies* however I may be blamed

BLACK KNIGHT
   If both Bishops had been there for seconds   225
'T 'ad been a complete duel.
WHITE KING   Then thou heard'st
The violence intended.
BLACK QUEEN'S PAWN   'T is a truth
I joy to justify. I was an agent, sir,
On virtue's part, and raised that confused noise
That startled his attempt, and gave her liberty.   230
WHITE QUEEN'S PAWN
   Oh 't is a righteous story she has told, sir,
My life and fame stand mutually engaged,
Both to the truth and goodness of this Pawn.
WHITE KING
   Does it appear to you yet: clear as the sun?
BLACK KNIGHT
   'Las, I believed it long before 't was done.   235
BLACK KING
   Degenerate
BLACK QUEEN   Base
BLACK BISHOP   Perfidious
BLACK DUKE   Traitorous Pawn!
BLACK QUEEN'S PAWN
   What, are you all beside yourselves?
BLACK KNIGHT   But I.
Remember that, Pawn!
BLACK QUEEN'S PAWN   May a fearful barrenness
Blast both my hopes and pleasures, if I brought not
Her ruin in my pity, a new trap   240
For her more sure confusion.
BLACK KNIGHT   Have I won now?
Did I not say 't was craft and machination?
I smelt conspiracy all the way it went
Although the mess were covered, I'm so used to it.
BLACK KING
   That Queen would I fain finger.
BLACK KNIGHT   You're too hot, sir,   245
If she were took, the game would be ours quickly.
My aim's at that White Knight, entrap him first
The Duke will follow too.
BLACK BISHOP   I would that Bishop
Were in my diocese, I'd soon change his whiteness.
BLACK KNIGHT
   Sir, I could whip you up a Pawn immediately;   250

I know where my game stands.

BLACK KING   Do it suddenly:
Advantage least must not be lost in this play.

BLACK KNIGHT
 [*Seizes* WHITE KING'S PAWN] Pawn, thou art ours.

WHITE KNIGHT   He's
                                    taken by default,
By wilful negligence. Guard the sacred persons,
Look well to the White Bishop, for that Pawn   255
Gave guard to the Queen and him in the third place.

BLACK KNIGHT
 See what sure piece you lock your confidence in.
I made this Pawn here by corruption ours,
As soon as honour by creation yours;
This whiteness upon him is but the leprosy   260
Of pure dissimulation. View him now:
His heart, and his intents are of our colour.

 [*His upper garment taken off, he appears Black underneath*]

WHITE KNIGHT
 Most dangerous hypocrite.

WHITE QUEEN   One made against us.

WHITE DUKE
 His truth of their complexion!

WHITE KING   Has my goodness,
Clemency, love, and favour gracious raised thee   265
From a condition next to popular labour,

262 s.d. B T omits

253–277 The whole passage can best be interpreted as referring to the Earl
    of Middlesex and his conviction for peculation.
255–256 This is obscure both as chess and as allegory. Does 'the third place'
    refer to the third rank of the board? And why should the King's Pawn
    be particularly associated with the protection of the Queen and the
    Bishop? Perhaps one is merely to imagine a literal chess position in
    which these two pieces were protected by a Pawn which has now been
    captured.
264–269 The central lines in this passage, 266–268, are omitted in A, an
    indication that Middleton's endeavour to make the White King's Pawn
    resemble Lionel Cranfield, the Earl of Middlesex, was a late idea
    (Middlesex was born poor and rose from city apprentice to Lord
    Treasurer). Line 269 has been interpreted as referring either to Cran-
    field's elevation to the peerage or to his marriage to a relation of
    Buckingham's; but since it is in A, it was apparently intended to be
    taken in a general sense.

Took thee from all the dubitable hazards
Of fortune, her most unsecure adventures,
And grafted thee into a branch of honour,
And dost thou fall from the top-bough by the rottenness   270
Of thy alone corruption, like a fruit
That's over-ripened by the beams of favour?
Let thy own weight reward thee, I have forgot thee;
Integrity of life is so dear to me
Where I find falsehood or a crying trespass,   275
Be it in any whom our grace shines most on,
I'd tear 'em from my heart.
WHITE BISHOP   Spoke like heaven's substitute.
WHITE KING
    You have him, we can spare him, and his shame
    Will make the rest look better to their game.
BLACK KNIGHT
    The more cunning we must use then.
BLACK KING   We shall match you,   280
    Play how you can, perhaps and mate you too.
FAT BISHOP
    Is there so much amazement spent on him
    That's but half black? There might be hope of that man;
    But how will this House wonder if I stand forth
    And show a whole one, instantly discover   285
    One that's all black where there's no hope at all?
WHITE KING
    I'll say thy heart then justifies thy books;
    I long for that discovery.
FAT BISHOP   Look no farder then,
    Bear witness all the House I am the man
    And turn myself into the Black House freely;   290
    I am of this side now.
WHITE KNIGHT   Monster ne'er matched him!
BLACK KING
    This is your noble work, Knight.
BLACK KNIGHT   Now I'll halter him.
FAT BISHOP
    Next news you hear expect my books against you
    Printed at Douay, Brussels, or Spoletta.

292 *halter* hang

282–304 Omitted in A. Cf. notes on II.ii, 1 and III.i, 1–79.
294 'Most of the Jesuits' books were printed at Douay, Brussels, Rheims,
    Paris, and St. Omer; none, however, at Spalatro' (Bullen).

WHITE KING
    See his goods seized on.
FAT BISHOP   'Las, they were all conveyed   295
    Last night by water to a tailor's house,
    A friend of the Black cause.
WHITE KNIGHT   A prepared hypocrite.
WHITE DUKE
    Premeditated turncoat.
    [*Exeunt* WHITE KING, QUEEN, BISHOP, KNIGHT, *and* DUKE]
FAT BISHOP   Yes, rail on,
    I'll reach you in my writings when I'm gone.
BLACK KNIGHT
    Flatter him a while with honours, till we put him   300
    Upon some dangerous service and then burn him.
BLACK KING
    This came unlooked for.
BLACK DUKE   How we joy to see you.
FAT BISHOP
    Now I'll discover all the White House to you.
BLACK DUKE
    Indeed! That will both reconcile and raise you.
    [*Exeunt* BLACK KING, BLACK QUEEN, BLACK DUKE, BLACK
                        BISHOP *and* FAT BISHOP]
WHITE KING'S PAWN
    I rest upon you, Knight, for my advancement.   305
BLACK KNIGHT
    Oh, for the staff, the strong staff that will hold,
    And the red hat fit for the guilty mazzard?
    Into the empty bag know thy first way,
    Pawns that are lost are ever out of play.
WHITE KING'S PAWN
    How's this?
BLACK KNIGHT   No replications, you know me,   310
    No doubt ere long you'll have more company;

298 s.d. Qq T omits
307 *mazzard* head   310 *replications* replies

295–297 De Dominis attempted to smuggle his acquisitions out of England
    in an ambassador's train, but they were seized.
301 De Dominis was posthumously convicted of heresy, his body disinterred
    and burnt.
309 Unlike captured pieces, Pawns cannot be 'resurrected' by the rule of
    'promotion'.

[Puts WHITE KING'S PAWN *into the bag]*

The bag is big enough, 't will hold us all.

Exeunt [BLACK KNIGHT *and* BLACK KNIGHT'S PAWN]

WHITE QUEEN'S PAWN
 I sue to thee, prithee be one of us,
 Let my love win thee. Thou hast done truth this day,
 And yesterday my honour noble service;   315
 The best Pawn of our House could not transcend it.

BLACK QUEEN'S PAWN
 My pity flamed with zeal, especially
 When I foresaw your marriage, then it mounted.

WHITE QUEEN'S PAWN
 How, marriage!

BLACK QUEEN'S PAWN That contaminating act
 Would have spoiled all your fortunes—a rape! bless us all! 320

WHITE QUEEN'S PAWN
 Thou talk'st of marriage.

BLACK QUEEN'S PAWN   Yes, yes, you do marry,
 I saw the man.

WHITE QUEEN'S PAWN The man!

BLACK QUEEN'S PAWN
 An absolute handsome gentleman, a complete one,
 You'll say so when you see him, heir to three red hats
 Besides his general hopes in the Black House.   325

WHITE QUEEN'S PAWN
 Why, sure you're much mistaken for this man;
 Why, I have promised single life to all my affections.

BLACK QUEEN'S PAWN
 Promise you what you will, or I, or all of us,
 There's a fate rules and overrules us all, methinks.

WHITE QUEEN'S PAWN
 Why how came you to see, or know this mystery! 330

BLACK QUEEN'S PAWN
 A magical glass I bought of an Egyptian
 Whose stone retains that speculative virtue

---

323 *absolute* perfectly
332 *speculative* having power to show visions

---

317 'This second attack on the White Queen's Pawn is pure allegory: in
 detail it has no reference to the particular events in the second invasion
 of the Palatinate; in general it is meant to symbolize Maximilian's desire
 to unite the Palatinate with his dukedom of Bavaria' (Morris, *op. cit.*,
 p. 51).

Presented the man to me. Your name brings him
As often as I use it, and methinks
I never have enough, person and postures   335
Are all so pleasing.
WHITE QUEEN'S PAWN   This is wondrous strange.
The faculties of soul are still the same,
I can feel no one motion tend that way.
BLACK QUEEN'S PAWN
We do not always feel our faith we live by,
Nor ever see our growth, yet both work upward.   340
WHITE QUEEN'S PAWN
'T was well applied, but may I see him?
BLACK QUEEN'S PAWN
Surely you may without all doubt or fear,
Observing the right use as I was taught it,
Not looking back or questioning the spectre.
WHITE QUEEN'S PAWN
That's no hard observation, trust it with me.   345
Is't possible? I long to see this man.
BLACK QUEEN'S PAWN
Pray follow me then and I'll ease you instantly.

Exeunt

Act III, Scene ii

Enter a BLACK JESTING PAWN

BLACK JESTING PAWN
I would so fain take one of these White Pawns now,
I'd make him do all under-drudgery,
Feed him with asses' milk crumbled with goats' cheese,
And all the whitemeats could be devised for him,
I'd make him my white jennet when I pranced 't   5
After the Black Knight's litter.

Enter a WHITE PAWN

338 *motion* impulse
343 *Observing . . . use* if you observe the proper procedure
345 *hard observation* difficult rule
  3 *crumbled* thickened
  4 *whitemeats* dishes made with milk and eggs
  5 *pranced't* ed. T prauncst

---

  6 *Black . . . litter.* Gondomar's actual litter, famous in London, was
  obtained for use in the play. See note on I.i, 243 s.d.

WHITE PAWN   And you would look then
   Just like the devil striding o'er a nightmare
   Made of a miller's daughter.
BLACK JESTING PAWN   A pox on you,
   Were you so near? I'm taken like a black-bird
   In the great snow, this White Pawn grinning over me.   10
WHITE PAWN
   And now because I will not foul my clothes
   Ever hereafter, for white quickly soils, you know—
BLACK JESTING PAWN
   I prithee get thee gone then, I shall smut thee.
WHITE PAWN
   Nay, I'll put that to venture now I have snapped thee,
   Thou shalt do all the dirty drudgery   15
   That slavery was e'er put to.
BLACK JESTING PAWN   I shall cozen you:
   You may chance come and find your work undone then,
   For I'm too proud to labour—I'll starve first,
   I tell you that beforehand.
WHITE PAWN   I will fit you then
   With a black whip that shall not be behind-hand.   20
BLACK JESTING PAWN
   Pugh, I have been used to whipping, I have whipped
   Myself three mile out of town in a morning; and
   I can fast a fortnight and make all your meat
   Stink and lie on your hands!
WHITE PAWN
   To prevent that your food shall be blackberries,   25
   And upon gaudy-days a pickled spider
   Cut like an anchovis; I'm not to learn
   A monkey's ordinary. Come, sir, will you frisk?

Enter a second BLACK PAWN

SECOND BLACK PAWN
   Soft, soft you; you have no such bargain of it,
   If you look well about you.
WHITE PAWN   By this hand,   30
   I am snapt too, a Black Pawn in the breech of me.

11 speech heading omitted in T
14 *venture* trial
21–22 lineation ed.
26 *gaudy-days* festival days
27 *anchovis* anchovy
28 *ordinary* diet

We three look like a birdspit, a white chick
Between two russet woodcocks.
BLACK JESTING PAWN   I'm so glad of this.
WHITE PAWN
    But you shall have small cause, for I'll firk you.
SECOND BLACK PAWN
    Then I'll firk you again.
WHITE PAWN   And I'll firk him again.   35
BLACK JESTING PAWN
    Mass, here will be old firking; I shall have
The worst on't; I can firk nobody.
We draw together now for all the world
Like three flies with one straw through their buttocks. [*Exeunt*]

Act III, Scene iii

Enter BLACK QUEEN'S PAWN *and* WHITE QUEEN'S PAWN

BLACK QUEEN'S PAWN
    This is the room he did appear to me in;
And look you, this the magic glass that showed him.
WHITE QUEEN'S PAWN
    I find no motion yet, what should I think on't?
A sudden fear invades me, a faint trembling
Under this omen,   5
As is oft felt the panting of a turtle
Under a stroking hand.
BLACK QUEEN'S PAWN   That bodes good luck still,
Sign you shall change state speedily, for that trembling
Is always the first symptom of a bride.
For any vainer fears that may accompany   10
His apparition, by my truth to friendship
I quit you of the least. Never was object
More gracefully presented, the very air
Conspires to do him honour, and creates
Sweet vocal sounds as if a bridegroom entered,   15
Which argues the blest harmony of your loves.

34 *firk* trounce
36 *old* plenty of
37–39 lineation ed.
6 *turtle* turtle dove

---

1 This scene may have been suggested by the episode of Merlin's mirror
in *The Faerie Queene*, Bk. III, canto II. But Act II of Rowley's *A
Shoemaker a Gentleman* also provides a close parallel.

WHITE QUEEN'S PAWN
   And will the using of my name produce him?
BLACK QUEEN'S PAWN
   Nay of yours only, else the wonder halted.
To clear you of that doubt I'll put the difference
In practice, the first thing I do, and make   20
His invocation in the name of others.
WHITE QUEEN'S PAWN
   'T will satisfy me much, that.
BLACK QUEEN'S PAWN   It shall be done.
      Thou, whose gentle form and face
      Filled lately this Egyptic glass,
      By the imperious powerful name   25
      And the universal fame
      Of the mighty Black House Queen,
      I conjure thee to be seen.
What! See you nothing yet?
WHITE QUEEN'S PAWN   Not any part;
   Pray, try another.
BLACK QUEEN'S PAWN   You shall have your will.   30
      I double my command and power
      And at the instant of this hour
      Invoke thee in the White Queen's name,
      With stay for time, and shape the same.
What see you yet?
WHITE QUEEN'S PAWN   There's nothing shows at all.   35
BLACK QUEEN'S PAWN
   My truth reflects the clearer then; now fix
And bless your fair eyes with your own forever.
      Thou well-composed, by fate's hand drawn
      To enjoy the White Queen's Pawn,
      Of whom thou shalt (by virtue met)   40
      Many graceful issues get,
      By the beauty of her fame,
      By the whiteness of her name,
      By her fair and fruitful love,
      By her truth that mates the dove,   45
      By the meekness of her mind,
      By the softness of her kind,

18 *else . . . halted* otherwise there would be nothing strange
34 *With . . . same* i.e., appear as you did previously and remain
36 *Black Queen's Pawn* ed. T assigns to Black Bishop's Pawn
45 *mates* equals that of
47 *kind* nature

    By the lustre of her grace,
      By all these thou art summoned to this place.
Hark, how the air, enchanted with your praises   50
And his approach, those words to sweet notes raises.

Music. Enter the Jesuit in rich attire like an apparition;
presents himself before the glass; then exit

WHITE QUEEN'S PAWN
    Oh let him stay a while, a little longer!
BLACK QUEEN'S PAWN
    That's a good hearing.
WHITE QUEEN'S PAWN
    If he be mine why should he part so soon?
BLACK QUEEN'S PAWN
    Why this is but the shadow of yours. How do you?   55
WHITE QUEEN'S PAWN
    Oh I did ill to give consent to see it.
What certainty is in our blood or state?
What we still write is blotted out by fate;
Our wills are like a cause that is law-tossed,
What one court orders is by another crossed.   60
BLACK QUEEN'S PAWN
    I find no fit place for this passion here,
'T is merely an intruder. He is a gentleman
Most wishfully composed; honour grows on him
And wealth piled up for him; h'as youth enough, too,
And yet in the sobriety of his countenance   65
Grave as a tetrarch, which is gracious
In the eye of modest pleasure. Where's the emptiness?
What can you more request?
WHITE QUEEN'S PAWN   I do not know
What answer yet to make! It does require
A meeting 'twixt my fear and my desire.   70

53 *That's . . . hearing* that's good to hear
54 *part* depart
60 *crossed* denied, thwarted
61 *passion* complaint, sorrow
62 *merely* wholly
63 *wishfully composed* formed just as one would wish
66 *tetrarch* governor of a Roman province

---

51 s.d. As Bald points out, it is clear from the phrase '*before* the glass' and
    from the warning at III.i, 344 that there must be no 'looking back or
    questioning the spectre' that the Jesuit comes onto the stage behind
    the White Queen's Pawn so that she sees him reflected in the mirror.

BLACK QUEEN'S PAWN
   [*Aside*] She's caught, and which is strange, by her most
                      wronger. [*Exeunt*]

Act IV, Scene i

Enter BLACK KNIGHT'S PAWN *meeting the* BLACK
BISHOP'S PAWN *richly accoutred*

BLACK KNIGHT'S PAWN
   [*Aside*] 'T is he, my confessor! He might ha' passed me
   Seven years together, had I not by chance
   Advanced mine eye upon that lettered hatband,
   The Jesuitical symbol to be known by,
   Worn by the brave collegians by consent.   5
   'T is a strange habit for a holy father,
   A president of poverty especially;
   But we, the sons and daughters of obedience,
   Dare not once think awry, but must confess ourselves
   As humbly to the father of that feather,   10
   Long spur and poniard, as to the albe and altar,
   And happy we're so highly graced to attain to it.—
   Holy and reverend!
BLACK BISHOP'S PAWN   How! Hast found me out?
BLACK KNIGHT'S PAWN
   Oh sir, put on the sparkling'st trim of glory,
   Perfection will shine foremost, and I knew you   15
   By the catholical mark you wear about you,
   The mark above your forehead.
BLACK BISHOP'S PAWN   Are you grown
   So ambitious in your observance? Well, your business?
   I have my game to follow.
BLACK KNIGHT'S PAWN   I have a worm
   Follows me so that I can follow no game;   20
   The most faint-hearted Pawn, if he could see his play,
   Might snap me up at pleasure. I desire, sir,

6 *'T is a strange* Q3 This a strange T
16 *catholical mark* the lettered hat-band
19 *worm* pang of conscience

1–12 The Jesuits were said to go about disguised, sometimes richly
   costumed as gallants, but, according to Gee, they 'have the superlative
   cognizance whereby they know one another; and that is, as I observed
   from this time, a gold hat-band studded with letters or characters'.
   Foote Out of the Snare, p. 69.

To be absolved; my conscience being at ease,
I could then with more courage ply my game.
BLACK BISHOP'S PAWN
    'T was a base fact.
BLACK KNIGHT'S PAWN   'T was to a schismatic Pawn, sir.   25
BLACK BISHOP'S PAWN
    What's that to the nobility of revenge?
    Suffices, I have neither will nor power
    To give you absolution for that violence.
    Make your petition to the Penance-chamber.
    If the tax-register relieve you in't   30
    By the Black Bishop's clemency, you have wrought out
    A singular piece of favour with your money;
    That's all your refuge now.
BLACK KNIGHT'S PAWN   This sting shoots deeper. [*Exit*]
BLACK BISHOP'S PAWN
    Yonder's my game, which, like a politic chess-master,
    I must not seem to see.

        Enter WHITE QUEEN'S PAWN *and* BLACK QUEEN'S PAWN

WHITE QUEEN'S PAWN   Oh my heart!   35
BLACK QUEEN'S PAWN
    That 't is!
WHITE QUEEN'S PAWN
    The very self-same that the magical mirror
    Presented lately to me.
BLACK QUEEN'S PAWN   And how like
    A most regardless stranger he walks by,
    Merely ignorant of his fate; you are not minded   40
    The principal'st part of him. What strange mysteries
    Inscrutable love works by!
WHITE QUEEN'S PAWN   The time you see
    Is not yet come!
BLACK QUEEN'S PAWN   But 't is in our power now
    To bring time nearer—knowledge is a mastery—

25 *fact* action
26 *What's . . . revenge* i.e., what's that in comparison to the baseness
    of the revenge that you took
30 *If . . . in't* if you can buy absolution
33 *all your* your only
39 *regardless* indifferent
40 *Merely* wholly
40–41 *minded . . . him* present in his mind
44 *mastery* power

And make it observe us, and not we it.   45

WHITE QUEEN'S PAWN
    I would force nothing from its proper virtue,
Let time have his full course; I'd rather die
The modest death of undiscovered love
Than have heaven's least and lowest servant suffer
Or in his motion receive check for me.   50
How is my soul's growth altered, that single life,
The fittest garment that peace ever made for't,
Is grown too straight, too stubborn on the sudden.

BLACK QUEEN'S PAWN
    He comes this way again.

WHITE QUEEN'S PAWN   Oh there's a traitor
Leaped from my heart into my cheek already   55
That will betray all to his powerful eye
If it but glance upon me.

BLACK QUEEN'S PAWN   By my verity,
Look, he's passed by again, drowned in neglect
Without the prosperous hint of so much happiness
To look upon his fortunes. How close fate   60
Seals up the eye of human understanding,
Till like the sun-flower time and love uncloses it.
'T were pity he should dwell in ignorance longer.

WHITE QUEEN'S PAWN
    What will you do?

BLACK QUEEN'S PAWN   Yes, die a bashful death, do,
And let the remedy pass by unused still.   65
You are changed enough already an you'd look into it.—
Absolute sir, with your most noble pardon
For this my rude intrusion, I am bold
To bring the knowledge of a secret nearer
By many days, sir, than it would arrive   70
In its own proper revelation with you.
Pray turn and fix: do you know yon noble goodness?

BLACK BISHOP'S PAWN
    'T is the first minute my eye blest me with her,
And clearly shows how much my knowledge wanted,
Not knowing her till now.

---

45 *observe* wait upon, obey
46 *proper virtue* true nature
50 *motion* natural course
53 *straight . . . stubborn* tight . . . stiff
66 *an* (i.e., if) ed. T and
67 *Absolute* very noble   72 *fix* fix your gaze, look

BLACK QUEEN'S PAWN She's to be liked then? 75
Pray view advisedly; there is strong reason
That I'm so bold to urge it, you must guess;
The work concerns you nearer than you think for.
BLACK BISHOP'S PAWN
Her glory, and the wonder of this secret
Puts a reciprocal amazement on me. 80
BLACK QUEEN'S PAWN
And 't is not without worth; you two must be
Better acquainted.
BLACK BISHOP'S PAWN Is there cause? Affinity?
Or any courteous help creation joys in
To bring that forward?
BLACK QUEEN'S PAWN Yes, yes, I can show you
The nearest way to that perfection 85
(Of a most virtuous one) that joy e'er found.
Pray mark her once again, then follow me
And I will show you her must be your wife, sir.
BLACK BISHOP'S PAWN
The mystery extends, or else creation
Has set that admirable piece before us 90
To choose our chaste delights by.
BLACK QUEEN'S PAWN Please you follow, sir.
BLACK BISHOP'S PAWN
What art have you to put me on an object
And cannot get me off? 'T is pain to part from it.
                    Exit [*with* BLACK QUEEN'S PAWN]
WHITE QUEEN'S PAWN
If there prove no check in that magical glass,
But my proportion come as fair and full 95
Into his eye as his into mine lately,
Then I'm confirmed he is mine own forever.

Enter again [BLACK QUEEN'S PAWN *and* BLACK BISHOP'S
                    PAWN]
BLACK BISHOP'S PAWN
The very self-same that the mirror blest me with,

75 *to be liked* likable, attractive
82–83 *Affinity . . . in* i.e., are we in any way related?
85–86 *perfection . . . one* i.e., the relation of marriage
89–91 i.e., that mystifies me further, unless you mean that she is the
    ideal with reference to which I must choose a wife
92–93 *put . . . off* give me a goal without enabling me to attain it
95 *proportion* figure, appearance
98–99 lineation ed.

From head to foot, the beauty and the habit.
Kept you this place still? Did you not remove, lady?   100

WHITE QUEEN'S PAWN
     Not a foot farder, sir.

BLACK BISHOP'S PAWN   Is 't possible?
I would have sworn I'd seen the substance yonder,
'T was to that lustre, to that life presented.

WHITE QUEEN'S PAWN
     E'en so was yours to me, sir.

BLACK BISHOP'S PAWN   Saw you mine?

WHITE QUEEN'S PAWN
     Perfectly clear, no sooner my name used   105
But yours appeared.

BLACK BISHOP'S PAWN Just so did yours at mine now.

BLACK QUEEN'S PAWN
     Why stand you idle? Will you let time cozen you,
Protracting time, of those delicious benefits
That fate hath marked to you, you modest pair
Of blushing gamesters—and you, sir, the bashfulest,   110
I cannot flatter a foul fault in any—
Can you be more than man and wife assigned,
And by a power the most irrevocable?
Others that be adventurers in delight
May meet with crosses, shame, or separation,   115
Their fortunes hid, and the events locked from 'em;
You know the mind of fate, you must be coupled.

BLACK BISHOP'S PAWN
     She speaks but truth in this. I see no reason then,
That we should miss the relish of this night
But that we are both shamefaced.

WHITE QUEEN'S PAWN   How? This night, sir?   120
Did not I know you must be mine, and therein
Your privilege runs strong, for that loose motion
You never should be. Is it not my fortune
To match with a pure mind, then I am miserable.
The doves and all chaste loving winged creatures   125
Have their pairs fit, their desires justly mated;

102 *substance* the real thing
107 *cozen* cheat
108 *Protracting* delaying
111 *flatter* condone for purposes of flattery
115 *crosses* frustrations, impediments
122 *motion* proposal
126 *pairs* mates

Is woman more unfortunate? A virgin,
The May of woman! Fate that has ordained, sir,
We should be man and wife, has not given warrant
For any act of knowledge till we are so.   130
BLACK BISHOP'S PAWN
    Tender-eyed modesty, how it grieves at this!
    [*Aside to* BLACK QUEEN'S PAWN] I'm as far off for all this
                                        strange imposture
    As at first interview. Where lies our game now?
    You know I cannot marry by my order.
BLACK QUEEN'S PAWN
    I know you cannot, sir, yet you may venture   135
    Upon a contract.
BLACK BISHOP'S PAWN   Hah!
BLACK QUEEN'S PAWN   Surely you may, sir,
    Without all question so far, without danger
    Or any stain to your vow, and that may take her.
    Nay, do't with speed; she'll think you mean the better, too.
BLACK BISHOP'S PAWN
    [*To* WHITE QUEEN'S PAWN] Be not too lavish of that
                                        blessed spring; 140
    Y'ave wasted that upon a cold occasion now
    Would wash a sinful soul white. By our love-joys,
    That motion shall ne'er light upon my tongue more
    Till we're contracted, then I hope y'are mine.
WHITE QUEEN'S PAWN
    In all just duty ever.
BLACK QUEEN'S PAWN   Then? Do you question it?   145
    Push, then y'are man and wife, all but church ceremony.
    Pray let's see that done first; she shall do reason then.—
    [*Aside*] Now I'll enjoy the sport and cozen you both,
    My blood's game is the wages I have worked for. *Exeunt*

131 *grieves* Q1, Q2 T gives
132 *strange imposture* sly pretence
141 *cold occasion* occasion when there was no necessity for weeping
149 *blood's* passion's

---

136 *contract.* That is, 'pre-contract' or formal betrothal. For the extent to
    which this 'hand-fasting' was considered as equivalent to a legally valid
    marriage without the necessity of a religious ceremony see the numerous
    discussions of *Measure for Measure*, I.ii, 141–145 (e.g., *Shakespeare's
    England*, ed. Sir Walter Raleigh, I, 407–408). The casuistry here, of
    course, is that a priest who entered upon such a 'pre-contract' was
    binding himself to two contradictory vows.

Act IV, Scene ii

Enter BLACK KNIGHT *with his* PAWN

BLACK KNIGHT
 Pawn, I have spoken to the Fat Bishop for thee,
 I'll get thee absolution from his own mouth.
 Reach me my chair of ease, my chair of cozenage;
 Seven thousand pound in women, reach me that.
 I love a' life to sit upon a bank   5
 Of heretic gold. Oh soft and gentle, sirrah!
 There's a foul flaw in the bottom of my drum, Pawn.
 I ne'er shall make sound soldier, but sound treacher
 With any he in Europe. How now, qualm?
 Thou hast the puking'st soul that e'er I met with, 10
 It cannot bear one suckling villainy.
 Mine can digest a monster without crudity,
 A sin as weighty as an elephant,
 And never wamble for 't.
BLACK KNIGHT'S PAWN
 Ay, you have been used to it, sir,   15
 That's a great help; the swallow of my conscience
 Has but a narrow passage you must think, yet
 It lies in the penitent pipe and will not down.
 If I had got seven thousand pound by offices
 And gulled down that, the bore would have been bigger. 20
BLACK KNIGHT
 Nay, if thou prove facetious I shall hug thee.
 Can a soft, rear, poor-poached iniquity
 So ride upon thy conscience? I'm ashamed of thee.
 Hadst thou betrayed the White House to the Black,
 Beggared a kingdom by dissimulation,   25
 Unjointed the fair frame of peace and traffic,
 Poisoned allegiance, set faith back, and wrought
 Women's soft souls e'en up to masculine malice
 To pursue truth to death if the cause roused 'em
 That stares and parrots are first taught to curse thee— 30

1 speech heading omitted in T
22 *rear* rare, undercooked
30 *stares* starlings

---

3 *chair of ease.* 'Golden Stool', A. Apparently Gondomar's chair of ease (a
chair with a hole cut in the seat, shown on the title page of Thomas
Scott's *The Second Part of Vox Populi*) was, like his litter, acquired by
the King's Men.

BLACK KNIGHT'S PAWN
   Ay, marry sir, here's swapping sins indeed.
BLACK KNIGHT
   All these, and ten times trebled, has this brain
Been parent to, they are my offsprings all.
BLACK KNIGHT'S PAWN
   A goodly brood!
BLACK KNIGHT   Yet I can jest as lightly,
Laugh and tell stirring stories to court madams   35
(Daughters of my seducement) with alacrity
As high and hearty as youth's time of innocence
That never knew a sin to shape a sorrow by.
I feel no tempest, not a leaf-wind stirring
To shake a fault; my conscience is becalmed rather.   40
BLACK KNIGHT'S PAWN
   I'm sure there is a whirlwind huffs in mine, sir.
BLACK KNIGHT
   Sirrah, I have sold the groom-o-the-stool six times,
And received money of six several ladies
Ambitious to take place of baronets' wives;
To three old mummy-matrons I have promised   45
The mothership o' the maids; I have taught our friends, too,
To convey White House gold to our Black Kingdom
In cold baked pasties and so cozen searchers.
For venting hallowed oil, beads, medals, pardons,
Pictures, Veronica's heads in private presses,   50
That's done by one i' th' habit of a pedlar,
Letters conveyed in rolls, tobacco-balls.
When a restraint comes, by my politic counsel
Some of our Jesuits turn gentlemen-ushers,

31 *swapping* huge
34 *as lightly* Q1, Q2 T *as tightly*
41 *huffs* blows
42 *groom . . . stool* office in the royal household
44 *place* precedence
45 *mummy* ancient, withered
46 *mothership . . . maids* post of supervisor of the royal maids
49 *venting* peddling
53 *restraint* policy of severity toward Roman Catholics
54 *gentlemen-ushers* school teachers

42–46 The whole of this passage is adapted, almost verbatim, from various
    sections of Thomas Scott's *The Second Part of Vox Populi* (see Bald,
    pp. 152–154). That this pamphlet was published subsequent to May
    1624 is evidence of the speed at which Middleton worked.

Some falconers, some park-keepers, and some huntsmen;   55
One took the shape of an old lady's cook once
And despatched two chares in a Sunday morning,
The altar and the dresser! Pray what use
Put I my summer recreation to?
But more to inform my knowledge in the state   60
And strength of the White Kingdom! No fortification,
Haven, creek, landing-place 'bout the White coast
But I got draught and platform, learned the depth
Of all their channels, knowledge of all sands,
Shelves, rocks, and rivers for invasion proper'st;   65
A catalogue of all the navy royal,
The burden of the ships, the brassy murderers,
The number of the men, to what cape bound;
Again, for the discovery of the inlands,
Never a shire but the state better known   70
To me than to the best inhabitants,
What power of men and horse, gentry's revenues,
Who well affected to our side, who ill,
Who neither well nor ill, all the neutrality.
Thirty-eight thousand souls have been seduced, Pawn,   75
Since the jails vomited with the pill I gave 'em.

BLACK KNIGHT'S PAWN
Sure you put oil of toad into that physic, sir.

BLACK KNIGHT
I'm now about a masterpiece of play
To entrap the White Knight and with false allurements
Entice him to the Black House—more will follow—   80
Whilst our Fat Bishop sets upon the Queen;
Then will our game lie sweetly.

Enter FAT BISHOP [*with a book*]

BLACK KNIGHT'S PAWN   He's come now, sir.

---

57 *chares* jobs
63 *platform* plan
65 *Shelves* reefs
67 *brassy murderers* pieces of ordinance
71 *best* Q3 brest T
73 *affected* disposed
77 *oil of toad* poison

---

76 See note on III.i, 87–97.

FAT BISHOP
    Here's *Taxa Poenitentiaria*, Knight,
    The book of general pardons of all prices,
    I have been searching for his sin this half hour   85
    And cannot light upon 't.
BLACK KNIGHT   That's strange, let me see it.
BLACK KNIGHT'S PAWN
    Pawn wretched that I am, has my rage done that
    There is no precedent of pardon for?
BLACK KNIGHT
    [*Reads*] 'For wilful murder thirteen pound four shillings
    And sixpence'—that's reasonable cheap—'For killing,   90
    Killing, killing, killing, killing, killing'—
    Why there's nothing but killing, Bishop, of this side.
FAT BISHOP
    Turn the sheet over, you shall find adultery
    And other trivial sins.
BLACK KNIGHT   Adultery? Oh,
    I'm in 't now.— [*Reads*] 'For adultery a couple   95
    Of shillings, and for fornication fivepence,'—
    Mass, those are two good pennyworths! I cannot
    See how a man can mend himself.—'For lying
    With mother, sister, and daughter'—ay, marry, sir—
    'Thirty-three pounds, three shillings, three pence,'—   100
    The sin's gradation right, paid all in threes too.
FAT BISHOP
    You have read the story of that monster, sir,
    That got his daughter, sister, and his wife
    Of his own mother—

83 *Taxa* the *Taxae Sacrae Poenitentiariae Apostolicae* which
    assigned the prices of absolution for various sins
85–86 lineation ed.
89–92 lineation ed.
97–100 lineation ed.
98 *mend himself* make a better bargain
101 *gradation right* in a correct proportion to the others

83–134 Bald suggests (p. 154) that Middleton probably knew one of the
    forged Protestant versions of the *Taxae*, such as the *Taxe des Parties
    Casuelles de la Boutique du Pape, au Latin & en Francois* . . . par A
    D[u] P[inet], A Lyon, 1564, which mentions all the sins mentioned in
    this passage. A full discussion of the various versions is found in Dr.
    Gibbings's *The Taxes of the Apostolic Penitentiary* (Dublin, 1872).
102 *story*. See the *Heptameron*, novel 30, and Bandello, *Nouvelle*, Pt. II,
    novel 35.

BLACK KNIGHT   [*Reads*] 'Simony, nine pound.'

FAT BISHOP
They may thank me for that, 't was nineteen   105
Before I came,
I have mitigated many of the sums.

BLACK KNIGHT
[*Reads*] 'Sodomy, sixpence.'—You should put that sum
Ever on the backside of your book, Bishop.

FAT BISHOP
There's few on 's very forward, sir.

BLACK KNIGHT   What's here, sir?   110
[*Reads*] 'Two old precedents of encouragement'—

FAT BISHOP
Ay, those are ancient notes.

BLACK KNIGHT
[*Reads*] 'Given as a gratuity for the killing of an heretical
prince with a poisoned knife, ducats five thousand.'

FAT BISHOP
True, sir, that was paid.   115

BLACK KNIGHT
[*Reads*] 'Promised also to Doctor Lopez for poisoning
the maiden Queen of the White Kingdom, ducats twenty
thousand; which said sum was afterwards given as a
meritorious alms to the nunnery at Lisbon, having at this
present ten thousand pound more at use in the townhouse of   120
Antwerp!'

BLACK KNIGHT'S PAWN
What's all this to my conscience, worthy holiness?
I sue for pardon, I have brought money with me.

FAT BISHOP
You must depart, you see there is no precedent
Of any price or pardon for your fact.   125

BLACK KNIGHT'S PAWN
Most miserable! Are fouler sins remitted?
Killing, nay, wilful murder?

FAT BISHOP   True, there's instance.

108–109 lineation ed.
125 *fact* deed
127 *instance* precedent

___

113–114 *heretical prince*. Either the assassination of Henri III of France by
Jacques Clement or of Henri IV by Ravaillac.
116 *Lopez*. Elizabeth I's Portuguese physician who was hanged in 1594
for accepting a bribe from Spain to poison her.

Were you to kill him I would pardon you;
There's precedent for that and price set down,
But none for gelding.   130
BLACK KNIGHT'S PAWN
     I have picked out understanding now forever
Out of that cabalistic bloody riddle:
I'll make away all my estate and kill him
And by that act obtain full absolution.   *Exit*

                Enter BLACK KING

BLACK KING
     Why Bishop! Knight! Where's your removes? Your traps?   135
Stand you now idle in the heat of game?
BLACK KNIGHT
     My life for yours, Black Sovereign, the game's ours;
I have wrought underhand for the White Knight
And his brave Duke and find 'em coming both.
FAT BISHOP
     Then for their sanctimonious Queen's surprisal   140
In this state-puzzle and distracted hurry
Trust my arch-subtlety with.
BLACK KING   Oh eagle pride!
Never was game more hopeful of our side.
BLACK KNIGHT
     [*Aside*] If Bishop Bull-beef be not snapt next bout
As the men stand, I'll never trust art more.   *Exeunt* 145

Act IV, Scene iii

[*Dumb show*]

Enter BLACK QUEEN'S PAWN *as conducting the* WHITE
to a chamber, then fetching in the BLACK BISHOP'S
PAWN, *the Jesuit, conveys him to another, puts out the
light, and she follows*

134 Q3 line omitted in T
135 speech heading omitted in T
     removes manoeuvres

144–145 Omitted in A.

Act IV, Scene iv

Enter WHITE KNIGHT *and* WHITE DUKE

WHITE KNIGHT
    True noble Duke, fair virtue's most endeared one,
    Let us prevent their rank insinuation
    With truth of cause and courage, meet their plots
    With confident goodness that shall strike 'em grovelling.

WHITE DUKE
    Sir, all the gins, traps and alluring snares   5
    The devil has been at work since '88 on
    Are laid for the great hope of this game only.

WHITE KNIGHT
    Why, the more noble will truth's triumph be;
    When they have wound about our constant courages
    The glittering'st serpent that e'er falsehood fashioned   10
    And glorying most in his resplendent poisons,
    Just heaven can find a bolt to bruise his head.

WHITE DUKE
    Look, would you see destruction lie a-sunning?

Enter BLACK KNIGHT

    In yonder smile sits blood and treachery basking,
    In that perfidious model of face-falsehood   15
    Hell is drawn grinning.

WHITE KNIGHT   What a pain it is
    For truth to fain a little.

BLACK KNIGHT   Oh fair Knight!
    The rising glory of that House of Candour,
    Have I so many protestations lost,
    Lost, lost, quite lost? Am I not worth your confidence?   20
    I that have vowed the faculties of soul,
    Life, spirit and brain to your sweet game of youth,
    Your noble fruitful game, can you mistrust
    Any foul play in me that have been ever
    The most submissive observer of your virtues   25
    And no way tainted with ambition

  1 *noble Duke* Q3 noble Knight T
  2 *prevent* anticipate
11 *his* Q1, Q2 their T
12 *bruise* ed. buize T
20–21 lineation ed.
23 *mistrust* suspect

Save only to be thought your first admirer?
How often have I changed for your delight
The royal presentation of my place
Into a mimic jester, and become   30
For your sake and the expulsion of sad thoughts
Of a grave state-sire a light son of pastime,
Made three score years a tomboy, a mere wanton?
I'll tell you what I told a Savoy dame once,
New wed, high, plump and lusting for an issue: 35
Within the year I promised her a child
If she could stride over St. Rumbant's breeches,
A relique kept at Mechlin. The next morning
One of my followers' old hose was conveyed
Into her chamber where she tried the feat,   40
By that and a court-friend after grew great.
WHITE KNIGHT
    Why who could be without thee?
BLACK KNIGHT   I will change
To any shape to please you, and my aim
Has been to win your love in all this game.
WHITE KNIGHT
    Thou hast it nobly, and we long to see   45
The Black House pleasure, state and dignity.
BLACK KNIGHT
    Of honour you'll so surfeit and delight
You'll ne'er desire again to see the White.   *Exeunt*

            Enter WHITE QUEEN

WHITE QUEEN
    My love, my hope, my dearest! Oh he's gone,
Ensnared, entrapped, surprised amongst the Black ones.   50
I never felt extremity like this;
Thick darkness dwells upon this hour, integrity
(Like one of heaven's bright luminaries now
By error's dullest elements interposed)

31 A, Q3 line omitted in T
33 *Made . . . tomboy* turned an old man into a child
41 *court-friend* lover
49–110 supplied from B, omitted in T

34–38 The source of this passage is doubtless the sentence from a discussion on the credibility of miracles which Bald quotes from *The
Second Part of Vox Populi*, p. 38: 'Nor that a young married wife shall
have a child in the same yeare if she can stride ouer at once Saint
Rombauts breeches at *Mechlin*.'

Suffer as black eclipse. I never was   55
More sick of love than now I am of horror.

Enter FAT BISHOP

I shall be taken, the game's lost, I'm set upon!
Oh 't is the turn-coat Bishop, having watched
The advantage of his play, comes now to seize on me.
Oh I'm hard beset, distressed, most miserable.   60

FAT BISHOP
        'T is vain to stir, remove which way you can
I take you now. This is the time we ever hoped for;
Queen, you must down.

WHITE QUEEN   No rescue, no deliverance?

FAT BISHOP
        The Black King's blood burns for thy prostitution
And nothing but the spring of thy chaste virtue   65
Can cool his inflammation; instantly
He dies upon a pleurisy of luxury
If he deflower thee not.

Enter WHITE BISHOP

WHITE QUEEN   Oh strait of misery!

WHITE BISHOP
        And is your holiness his divine procurer?

FAT BISHOP
        The devil's in 't, I'm taken by a ring-dove!   70
Where stood this Bishop that I saw him not?

WHITE BISHOP
        You were so ambitious you looked over me.
You aimed at no less person than the Queen,
The glory of the game; if she were won
The way were open to the master-check   75
Which—look you, he or his lives to give you;
Honour and virtue guide him in his station.

Enter WHITE KING

56 s.d. L omitted in B
63 *deliverance* ed. deliuererance B, deliverer L, Q1, Q2
67 *pleurisy* swelling
    luxury lust
70 *ring dove* wood pigeon, weakling
75 *master-check* checkmate

57–77 This passage is explained by Morris (*op. cit.*, p. 42) as referring to
    Queen Anne's conversion to the Church of Rome and Archbishop
    Abbot's claim to have obtained her death-bed recantation.

WHITE QUEEN
    Oh my safe sanctuary.
WHITE KING   Let heaven's blessings
  Be mine no longer than I am thy sure one,
  The dove's house is not safer in the rock   80
  Than thou in my firm bosom.
WHITE QUEEN   I am blessed in 't.
WHITE KING
    Is it that lump of rank ingratitude
  Swelled with the poison of hypocrisy?
  Could he be so malicious, has partaken   85
  Of the sweet fertile blessings of our kingdom?
  Bishop, thou hast done our White House gracious service
  And worthy the fair reverence of thy place.
  For thee, Black Holiness, that work'st out thy death
  As the blind mole, the proper'st son of earth,
  Who in the casting his ambitious hills up   90
  Is often taken, and destroyed in the midst
  Of his advanced work, 't were well with thee
  If like that verminous labourer, which thou imitat'st
  In hills of pride and malice, when death puts thee up
  The silent grave might prove thy bag forever,   95
  No deeper pit than that. For thy vain hope
  Of the White Knight, and his most firm assistant,
  Two princely pieces which I know thy thoughts
  Give lost forever now, my strong assurance
  Of their fixed virtues, could you let in seas   100
  Of populous untruths against that fort,
  'T would burst the proudest billows.
WHITE QUEEN   My fear's past then.
WHITE KING
    Fear? You were never guilty of an injury
  To goodness but in that.
WHITE QUEEN   It stayed not with me, sir.
WHITE KING
    It was too much if it usurped a thought;   105
  Place a good guard there.
WHITE QUEEN   Confidence is set, sir.
WHITE KING
    Take that prize hence, you reverend of men;
  Put covetousness into the bag again.

89 *proper'st* truest

82–85 Omitted in A.   109–110 Omitted in A.

FAT BISHOP
    The bag had need be sound, or it goes to wrack;
    Sin and my weight will make a strong one crack. [*Exeunt*] 110

Act V, Scene i

Music [BLACK BISHOP'S PAWN *discovered above*]. *Enter*
the BLACK KNIGHT *in his litter: calls*

BLACK KNIGHT
    Hold, hold!
    Is the Black Bishop's Pawn, the Jesuit,
    Planted above for his concise oration?
BLACK BISHOP'S PAWN
    Ecce triumphante me fixum Caesaris Arce.
BLACK KNIGHT
    Art there, my holy boy? Sirrah, Bishop Tumbrel   5
    Is snapped, in the bag by this time.
BLACK BISHOP'S PAWN
    Haeretici pereant sic!
BLACK KNIGHT
    All Latin! Sure the oration has infected him.
    Away, make haste, they're coming.

    Hautboys. Enter BLACK KING, [BLACK] QUEEN, [BLACK]
    DUKE *with* PAWNS, *meeting the* WHITE KNIGHT *and* DUKE

BLACK BISHOP'S PAWN
    Si quid mortalibus unquam oculis hilarem et gratum   10
    aperuit diem, si quid peramantibus amicorum animis
    gaudium attulit peperitive laetitiam, Eques Candidissime,
    praelucentissime, felicem profecto tuum a Domo Candoris
    ad Domum Nigritudinis accessum promisisse, peperisse,

110 *one* Q1, Q2 on B
    4 *triumphante* ed. triumphanti T 'Behold me fixed on Caesar's
        triumphal arch'
    5 *Tumbrel* dung cart
    7 'May all heretics perish so'
    14 *Nigritudinis* ed. Nigritutidinis T
        accessum ed. acces-accessum T

This scene represents the journey of Prince Charles and the Duke of
Buckingham to Madrid in 1623 to negotiate Charles's marriage with the
Infanta Maria.
1–9 Omitted in A. But the word 'litter' has been written in above the
    initial s.d., showing that the players had acquired Gondomar's litter
    after the date of A.

attulisse fatemur. Omnes adventus tui conflagrantissimi,   15
omni qua possumus laetitia, gaudio, congratulatione,
acclamatione, animis observantissimis, affectibus devotis-
simis, obsequiis venerabundis, te sospitem congratulamur.
BLACK KING
   Sir, in this short congratulatory speech
   You may conceive how the whole House affects you.   20
BLACK KNIGHT
   The colleges and sanctimonious seed-plots.
WHITE KNIGHT
   'T is clear, and so acknowledged, royal sir.
BLACK KNIGHT
   What honours, pleasures, rarities, delights
   Your noble thought can think—
BLACK QUEEN   Your fair eye fix on,
   That's comprehended in the spacious circle   25
   Of our Black Kingdom, they're your servants all.
WHITE KNIGHT
   How amply you endear us.
WHITE DUKE   They are favours
   That equally enrich the royal giver
   As the receiver in the free donation.
BLACK KNIGHT
   Hark, to enlarge your welcome, from all parts   30
   Is heard sweet sounding airs, abstruse things open
   Of voluntary freeness, and yond altar,
   The seat of adoration, seems to adore
   The virtues you bring with you.

17 *affectibus* ed. affectibur T	*devotissimis* ed. divotissimis T
20 *affects* has affection for	21 *colleges . . . plots* seminaries
22–29 supplied from B, omitted in T	25 *comprehended* included
27 *endear us* show us endeared	31 *abstruse* hidden

10–18 'If anything ever to mortal eyes opened a merry and welcome day, if
    anything ever brought joy to the most loving souls of friends, or begat
    happiness, most white and shining Knight, assuredly we confess that
    your happy arrival from the White House to the Black House has
    promised, has begotten, has brought it. All of us, most excited by your
    coming, with all gladness, joy, congratulation, and acclamation, with
    most respectful souls, most devoted feelings, and reverent allegiance,
    congratulate your safety.' (Translation from Brooke and Paradise.)
      This is an abridgement of an oration actually given by a Jesuit to
    Prince Charles during the visit to Spain. See George R. Price, 'The
    Latin Oration in *A Game at Chess*', *Huntington Library Quarterly*,
    XXIII (1960), 389–393.

WHITE KNIGHT   [*Aside*] There's a taste
Of the old vessel still, the erroneous relish.   35

Music. An altar discovered and statues,
with a song

Song

Wonder work some strange delight
This place was never yet without
To welcome the fair White House Knight,
And to bring our hopes about.
May from the altar flames aspire,   40
Those tapers set themselves afire.
May senseless things our joys approve
And those brazen statues move
Quickened by some power above,
Or what more strange, to show our love.   45

[*The images move in a dance*]

BLACK KNIGHT
A happy omen waits upon this hour;
All move portentously, the right-hand way.

BLACK KING
Come, let's set free all the most choice delights
That ever adorned days or quickened nights.   *Exeunt*

Act V, Scene ii

Enter WHITE QUEEN'S PAWN

WHITE QUEEN'S PAWN
I see 't was but a trial of my love now,
H'as a more modest mind, and in that virtue
Most worthily has fate provided for me.

34–35 *taste . . . relish* taint of popery
42 *approve* prove, feel
44 *Quickened* brought to life
45 *what . . . strange* anything that would be stranger still
   s.d. Qq omitted in T
46–47 s.d. Qq omitted in T
48 *Black King* ed. White King T

34–45 The White Knight's comment suggests that this episode is illus-
   trative of the Puritan hatred of Roman Catholic use of ornament and
   ritual.
47 *All . . . way.* That is, the dance goes clock-wise and thus toward the
   White House (see note on Induction, 52), a portent of amity.

Enter JESUIT

Hah! 't is the bad man in the reverend habit.
Dares he be seen again, traitor to holiness,   5
Oh marble-fronted impudence, and knows
How much he has wronged me? I'm ashamed he blushes not.

BLACK BISHOP'S PAWN

    Are you yet stored with any woman's pity?
Are you the mistress of so much devotion,
Kindness and charity, as to bestow   10
An alms of love on your poor sufferer yet
For your sake only?

WHITE QUEEN'S PAWN

    Sir, for the reverence and respect you ought
To give to sanctity, though none to me,
In being her servant vowed and wear her livery,   15
If I might counsel you, you should ne'er speak
The language of unchasteness in that habit,
You would not think how ill it does with you.
The world's a stage on which all parts are played:
You'd think it most absurd to have a devil   20
Presented there not in a devil's shape,
Or, wanting one, to send him out in yours;
You'd rail at that for an absurdity
No college e'er committed. For decorum's sake then,
For pity's cause, for sacred virtue's honour,   25
If you'll persist still in your devil's part,
Present him as you should do, and let one
That carries up the goodness of the play
Come in that habit, and I'll speak with him;
Then will the parts be fitted and the spectators   30
Know which is which. It must be strange cunning
To find it else, for such a one as you
Is able to deceive a mighty audience;
Nay, those you have seduced, if there be any
In the assembly, if they see what manner   35
You play your game with me, they cannot love you.
Is there so little hope of you to smile, sir?

5 *traitor to holiness* Q3 omitted in T
6 *fronted* browed
12 *White Queen's Pawn* ed. Black Queen's Pawn T
18 *does with* suits
28 *carries up* represents
31 *It . . . cunning* T They must have cunning judgments L, Q1, Q2
37 *to smile* that you can smile

BLACK BISHOP'S PAWN
    Yes, at your fears, at the ignorance of your power,
The little use you make of time, youth, fortune,
Knowing you have a husband for lust's shelter,   40
You dare not yet make bold with a friend's comfort;
This is the plague of weakness.
WHITE QUEEN'S PAWN   So hot-burning
The syllables of sin fly from his lips,
As if the letter came new cast from hell.
BLACK BISHOP'S PAWN
    Well, setting aside the dish you loathe so much,   45
Which has been heartily tasted by your betters,
I come to marry you to the gentleman
That last enjoyed you. 'Hope that pleases you,
There's no immodest relish in that office!
WHITE QUEEN'S PAWN
    [Aside] Strange of all others he should light on him,   50
To tie that holy knot that sought to undo me.—
Were you requested to perform that office?
BLACK BISHOP'S PAWN
    I name you a sure token.
WHITE QUEEN'S PAWN   As for that, sir—
Now y'are most welcome, and my fair hope's of you,
You'll never break the sacred knot you tie once   55
With any lewd solicitings hereafter.
BLACK BISHOP'S PAWN
    But all the craft's in getting of it knit,
You're all afire to make your cozening market;
I am the marrier and the man, do you know me?
Do you know me, nice iniquity, strict luxury,   60
And holy whoredom, that would clap on marriage
With all hot speed to solder up your game?
See what a scourge fate hath provided for thee:
You were a maid; swear still y'are no worse now,
I left you as I found you. Have I startled you?   65
I am quit with you now for my discovery,
Your outcries and your cunnings. Farewell, brokage!

42 *plague* ed. plauge T
49 *no . . . relish* nothing that smacks of immodesty
58 *market* bargain
60 *nice* bashful, fastidious   *luxury* lust
66 *quit* even
    my discovery revealing me
67 *brokage* trickery

WHITE QUEEN'S PAWN
     Nay, stay and hear me but give thanks a little,
If your ear can endure a work so gracious;
Then you may take your pleasure.
BLACK BISHOP'S PAWN   I have done that.   70
WHITE QUEEN'S PAWN
     That power that hath preserved me from this devil—
BLACK BISHOP'S PAWN
     How!
WHITE QUEEN'S PAWN
     This, that may challenge the chief chair in hell
And sit above his master—
BLACK BISHOP'S PAWN   Bring in merit!
WHITE QUEEN'S PAWN
     That suffered'st him through blind lust to be led,   75
Last night to the action of some common bed—
BLACK QUEEN'S PAWN
     (*Within*) Not over-common, neither!
BLACK BISHOP'S PAWN   Hah! what voice is
                                                       that?
WHITE QUEEN'S PAWN
     Of virgins be thou ever honoured:
Now you may go, you hear I have given thanks, sir.
BLACK BISHOP'S PAWN
     Here's a strange game! Did not I lie with you?   80
BLACK QUEEN'S PAWN
     (*Within*) No!
BLACK BISHOP'S PAWN
     What o' devil art thou?
WHITE QUEEN'S PAWN
     I will not answer you, sir,
After thanksgiving.
BLACK BISHOP'S PAWN   Why you made a promise to me
After the contract.
BLACK QUEEN'S PAWN   (*Within*) Yes.
BLACK BISHOP'S PAWN   A pox confound thee!   85
     I speak not to thee—and you were prepared for 't,
And set your joys more high—

76 *to . . . bed* to some prostitute
80 *Here's a strange game* Q3 This a strange game T Strange game
     indeed Q1, Q2
82 *o' devil* in the name of the devil
85 *After the contract* Q3 After thanksgiving T

BLACK QUEEN'S PAWN   (*Within*) Than you could
reach, sir.

BLACK BISHOP'S PAWN
Light, 't is a bawdy voice; I'll slit the throat on 't!

Enter BLACK QUEEN'S PAWN

BLACK QUEEN'S PAWN
What? Offer violence to your bedfellow?
To one that works so kindly, without rape?   90
BLACK BISHOP'S PAWN
My bedfellow?
BLACK QUEEN'S PAWN   Do you plant your scorn against me?
Why when I was probationer at Brussels
That engine was not known, then adoration
Filled up the place and wonder was in fashion.
Is 't turned to the wild seed of contempt so soon?   95
Can five years stamp a bawd? Pray look upon me,
I have youth enough to take it: 't is no more
Since you were chief agent for the transportation
Of ladies' daughters, if you be remembered.
Some of their portions I could name; who pursed 'em too. 100
They were soon dispossessed of worldly cares
That came into your fingers.
BLACK BISHOP'S PAWN   Shall I hear her?
BLACK QUEEN'S PAWN
Holy derision, yes, till thy ear swells
With thy own venom, thy profane life's vomit:
Whose niece was she you poisoned with child, twice,   105
Then gave her out possessed with a foul spirit
When 't was indeed your bastard?

Enter WHITE BISHOP'S PAWN *and* WHITE QUEEN

BLACK BISHOP'S PAWN   I am taken
In mine own toils.
WHITE BISHOP'S PAWN   Yes, and 't is just you should be.
WHITE QUEEN
And thou, lewd Pawn, the shame of womanhood.

88 *Light* By God's light
93 *engine* way of working

92–102 Bullen and Bald provide quotations from contemporary anti-
Catholic literature to show that at this point the Black Bishop's Pawn
is intended to represent Father John Floyd (or Flood) who was accused
of being the chief agent of the Jesuits for carrying English women to
convents on the Continent and depriving them of their possessions.

BLACK BISHOP'S PAWN
  I'm lost of all hands.
BLACK QUEEN'S PAWN   And I cannot feel   110
  The weight of my perdition now he's taken,
  'T is not the burden of a grasshopper.
BLACK BISHOP'S PAWN
  Thou whore of order, cockatrice *in voto*!

          Enter BLACK KNIGHT'S PAWN

BLACK KNIGHT'S PAWN
  Yond's the White Bishop's Pawn; have at his heart now.
WHITE QUEEN'S PAWN
  Hold, monster-impudence! Would'st thou heap a murder   115
  On thy first foul attempt? Oh merciless blood-hound,
  'T is time that thou wert taken.
BLACK KNIGHT'S PAWN   Death! Prevented!
WHITE QUEEN'S PAWN
  For thy sake, and yond partner in thy shame,
  I'll never know man farder than by name.   *Exeunt*

Act V, Scene iii

  Enter BLACK KING, [BLACK] QUEEN, [BLACK] DUKE,
  BLACK KNIGHT, [BLACK BISHOP], *with the* WHITE
              KNIGHT *and his* DUKE

WHITE KNIGHT
  Y'ave both enriched my knowledge, royal sir,
  And my content together.
BLACK KING   'Stead of riot
  We set you only welcome, surfeit is
  A thing that's seldom heard of in these parts.
WHITE KNIGHT
  I hear of the more virtue when I miss on 't.   5
BLACK KNIGHT
  We do not use to bury in our bellies

113 *cockatrice* cant term for harlot
115–117 lineation ed.
116 *Oh merciless bloodhound* A, Q3 omitted in T
119 *farder* further
  2 *riot* profligacy

  6–52 Bald argues (p. 157) that the mistakes in this passage noted by Dyce
      and Bullen are probably due to Middleton's hasty copying from a
      source that has not been traced. The whole passage is a satire on the
      Spaniards' parsimony noted by Charles and Buckingham.

Two hundred thousand ducats and then boast on 't,
Or exercise the old Roman painful-idleness
With care of fetching fishes far from home,
The golden-headed coracine out of Egypt,   10
The salpa from Eleusis, or the pelamis,
Which some call summer-whiting, from Chalcedon,
Salmons from Aquitaine, helops from Rhodes,
Cockles from Chios, franked and fatted up
With far and sapa, flour and cocted wine;   15
We cram no birds, nor Epicurean-like
Enclose some creeks of the sea, as Sergius Crata did,
He that invented the first stews for oysters
And other sea-fish, who, beside the pleasure
Of his own throat, got large revenues by th'invention   20
Whose fat example the nobility followed;
Nor do we imitate that arch-gormandizer,
With two and twenty courses at one dinner,
And betwixt every course he and his guests
Washed and used women, then sat down and strengthened,   25
Lust swimming in their dishes, which no sooner
Was tasted but was ready to be vented.

WHITE KNIGHT
    Most impious epicures!
BLACK KNIGHT   We commend rather,
Of two extremes, the parsimony of Pertinax
Who had half-lettuces set up to serve again;   30
Or his successor Julian that would make
Three meals of a lean hare, and often sup
With a green fig and wipe his beard, as we can.
The old bewailers of excess in those days

14 *franked* stuffed
15 *far* flour
    sapa boiled wine
    cocted boiled
17 *Crata* the correct Latin is 'Orata'
18 *stews* breeding beds
20–21 lineation ed.
24 *guests* ed. guesse T
25 *strengthened* ate more
28 speech heading omitted in T
29 *Pertinax* Roman Emperor (d. 193)
31 *Julian* Didius Julianus (d. 193)

31 *Julian.* Brooke and Paradise point out that Didius Julianus is here
confused with the abstemious Julian the Apostate.

Complained there was more coin bid for a cook   35
Than for a warhorse, but now cooks are purchased
After the rate of triumphs, and some dishes
After the rate of cooks; which must needs make
Some of your White House gormandizers, 'specially
Your wealthy, plump plebeians, like the hogs   40
Which Scaliger cites, that could not move for fat,
So insensible of either prick or goad,
That mice made holes to needle in their buttocks
And they ne'er felt 'em. There was once a ruler,
Cyrene's governor, choked with his own paunch,   45
Which death fat Sanctius, King of Castile, fearing
Through his infinite mass of belly, rather chose
To be killed suddenly, by a pernicious herb
Taken to make him lean, which old Corduba,
King of Morocco, counselled his fear to,   50
Than he would hazard to be stunk to death
As that huge cormorant that was choked before him.

WHITE KNIGHT
Well, you're as sound a spokesman, sir, for parsimony,
Clean abstinence, and scarce one meal a day,
As ever spoke with tongue.

BLACK KING   Censure him mildly, sir,   55
'T was but to find discourse.

BLACK QUEEN   He'll raise of anything.

WHITE KNIGHT
I shall be half afraid to feed hereafter.

WHITE DUKE
Or I, beshrew my heart, for I fear fatness,
The fog of fatness, as I fear a dragon,
The comeliness I wish for that's as glorious.   60

37 *triumphs* public shows
41 *Scaliger* Julius Caesar Scaliger (1484–1558)
43 *needle* bore
56 *raise* rayse T talk Q1, Q2
59 *fog* ed. fognes T

56 *raise* (rayse T). I have found no other example of this use of 'raise'.
  Brooke and Paradise emend to 'raise't'.
58–60 This is one of the two passages which make the question of Buckingham's role in this play confusing (cf. V.iii, 118–123 and Introduction,
  p. xiv). The theory that the Duke encouraged its production because it
  helped his political ends must take into account these passages in which,
  even if 'feigning a little', he confesses to weaknesses which were well
  known to be his.

WHITE KNIGHT
    Your course is wondrous strict; I should transgress sure,
Were I to change my side, as you have wrought me.
BLACK KNIGHT
    How you misprize! This is not meant to you-ward.
You that are wound up to the height of feeding
By clime and custom are dispensed withal;   65
You may eat kid, cabrito, calf and tons,
Eat and eat every day, twice if you please;
Nay, the franked hen, fattened with milk and corn,
A riot which the inhabitants of Delos
Were first inventors of, or the crammed cockle.   70
WHITE KNIGHT
    Well, for the food, I'm happily resolved on;
But for the diet of my disposition
There comes a trouble, you will hardly find
Food to please that.
BLACK KNIGHT   It must be a strange nature
We cannot find a dish for, having policy,   75
The master-cook of Christendom, to dress it;
Pray name your nature's diet.
WHITE KNIGHT   The first mess
Is hot ambition!
BLACK KNIGHT   That's but served in puff paste;
Alas, the meanest of our cardinals' cooks
Can dress that dinner. Your ambition, sir,   80
Can fetch no farder compass than the world?
WHITE KNIGHT
    That's certain, sir.
BLACK KNIGHT   We're about that already;
And in the large feast of our vast ambition
We count but the White Kingdom whence you came from

62 *wrought me* Qq wrought me to it T if I should change B
63 *misprize* misunderstand
   to you-ward to apply to you
64–65 *wound . . . custom* accustomed to good food by your nationality
66 *cabrito* lamb
   tons tunny fish
71 *happily . . . on* content
82 *about that* have begun on that

61–62 The White Knight ironically fears that he would never be able to
    sustain the asceticism preached by his Black counterpart. Here he
    begins, like Malcolm in *Macbeth* (IV.iii) to 'feign a little'.

The garden for our cook to pick his salads;   85
The food's lean France larded with Germany,
Before which comes the grave chaste signiory
Of Venice, served in capon-like in whitebroth;
From our chief oven, Italy, the bake-meats,
Savoy, the salt, Geneva, the chipped manchet;   90
Below the salt the Netherlands are placed,
A common dish at lower end a' the table
For meaner pride to fall to; for our second course
A spit of Portugals served in for plovers,
Indians and Moors for blackbirds; all this while   95
Holland stands ready melted, to make sauce
On all occasions; when the voider comes
And with such cheer our crammed hopes we suffice,
Zealand says grace, for fashion; then we rise.

WHITE KNIGHT
    Here's meat enough, a' conscience, for ambition!   100

BLACK KNIGHT
    If there be any want, there's Switzerland,
Polonia, and such pickled things will serve
To furnish out a table.

WHITE KNIGHT   You say well, sir;
But here's the misery: when I have stopped the mouth
Of one vice, there's another gapes for food;   105
I am as covetous as a barren womb,
The grave, or what's more ravenous.

BLACK KNIGHT   We are for you, sir;
Call you that heinous that's good husbandry?
Why we make money of our faiths, our prayers,
We make the very death-bed buy her comforts,   110
Most dearly pay for all her pious counsels,
Leave rich revenues for a few sale orisons
Or else they pass unreconciled without 'em.
Did you but view the vaults within our monasteries,
You'd swear then Plutus, which the fiction calls   115
The lord of riches, were entombed within 'em.

  90 *manchet* small loaf of wheaten bread
  91 *Below the salt* the inferior guests were placed below the principal
     salt cellar
  97 *voider* scrap-basket
  98 *cheer* entertainment, food
 100 *a' conscience* in all conscience
 112 *sale* tawdry
 113 *pass unreconciled* die unforgiven

BLACK DUKE
   You cannot pass for tuns!
WHITE KNIGHT   Is 't possible?
WHITE DUKE
   But how shall I bestow the vice I bring, sirs?
   You quite forget me, I shall be locked out
   By your strict key of life.
BLACK KNIGHT   Is yours so foul, sir?   120
WHITE DUKE
   Some that are pleased to make a wanton on 't
   Call it infirmity of blood, flesh-frailty,
   But certain there's a worse name in your books for 't.
BLACK KNIGHT
   The trifle of all vices, the mere innocent,
   The very novice of this house of clay: venery!   125
   If I but hug thee hard I show the worst on 't.
   'T is all the fruit we have here after supper;
   Nay, at the ruins of a nunnery once
   Six thousand infants' heads found in a fishpond.
WHITE KNIGHT
   How!   130
BLACK KNIGHT
   How? Ay, how? How came they thither, think you?
   Huldrick, bishop of Augsburg, in his Epistle
   To Nicholas the First, can tell you how;
   Maybe he was at cleansing of the pond;
   I can but smile to think how it would puzzle   135
   All mother-maids that ever lived in those parts
   To know their own child's head. But is this all?
BLACK DUKE
   Are you ours yet?
WHITE KNIGHT   One more, and I am silenced,
   But this that comes now will divide us, questionless;
   'T is ten times ten times worse than the forerunners.   140

117 speech heading omitted in T
    pass for tuns get through because of the wine casks
121 *make a wanton on't* dismiss lightly
125 *house of clay* body   139 *questionless* doubtless

118–123 Cf. note on V.iii, 58–60. Buckingham's reported conduct in Spain
    makes this passage seem double-edged. Bullen cites Sir Antony Welldon,
    The Court and Character of King James (1651), p. 146.
128–137 For discussion of a possible source of this passage see R. Southall,
    'A Missing Source-Book for Middleton's *A Game at Chesse*', *Notes &*
    Queries, IX (1960), 145–146.

BLACK KNIGHT
     Is it so vild there is no name ordained for 't?
     Toads have their titles, and creation gave
     Serpents and adders those names to be known by.
WHITE KNIGHT
     This of all others bears the hiddest venom,
     The smoothest poison,—I am an arch-dissembler, sir.   145
BLACK KNIGHT
     How!
WHITE KNIGHT   'T is my nature's brand; turn from me, sir;
     The time is yet to come that e'er I spake
     What my heart meant!
BLACK KNIGHT   And call you that a vice?
     Avoid all prophanation, I beseech you:
     The only prime state-virtue upon earth,   150
     The policy of empires! Oh take heed, sir,
     For fear it take displeasure and forsake you.
     It is a jewel of that precious value
     Whose worth's not known but to the skilful lapidary,
     The instrument that picks ope princes' hearts,   155
     And locks up ours from them with the same motion;
     You never yet came near our souls till now,
     Now y'are a brother to us; what we have done
     Has been dissemblance ever.
WHITE KNIGHT   There you lie then
     And the game's ours—we give thee checkmate by   160
     Discovery, King, the noblest mate of all.

               [*A great shout and flourish*]
BLACK KING
     I'm lost, I'm taken!
WHITE KNIGHT
     Ambitious, covetous, luxurious falsehood!

141 *vild* vile
144 *hiddest* most concealed
154–155 lineation ed.   161 s.d. Q1, Q2 omitted in T

160–161 The 'discovered mate' occurs when one piece moves out of the line
    of its fellow piece which thereby delivers an inescapable check. Here the
    Knight 'unmasks' the Rook. Saul's *Famous Game of Chesse-Play* (1614)
    calls the discovered mate 'the worthiest of all' (see Moore, *op. cit.*, p.
    766), presumably because it requires perfect co-operation between two
    pieces. Here the allegorical meaning is that Charles's pretended gulli-
    bility temporarily obscured Buckingham's penetration of the Spanish
    'plot'.

WHITE DUKE
   Dissembler includes all.
BLACK KING
   All hopes confounded!   165
BLACK QUEEN
   Miserable condition!

   Enter WHITE KING, [WHITE] QUEEN, [WHITE BISHOP,
       WHITE QUEEN'S PAWN, *and other*] WHITE PAWNS

WHITE KING
   Oh let me bless mine arms with this dear treasure,
   Truth's glorious masterpiece. See, Queen of sweetness,
   He's in my bosom safe, and yond fair structure
   Of comely honour, his true blessed assistant.   170
WHITE QUEEN
   May their integrities ever possess
   That peaceful sanctuary.
WHITE KNIGHT   As 't was a game, sir,
   Won with much hazard, so with much more triumph
   We gave him checkmate by discovery, sir.
WHITE KING
   Obscurity is now the fittest favour   175
   Falsehood can sue for, it well suits perdition;
   'T is their best course that so have lost their fame
   To put their heads into the bag for shame.

            The bag opens, the Black side in it

   And there behold the bag's mouth, like hell, opens
   To take her due, and the lost sons appear   180
   Greedily gaping for increase of fellowship
   In infamy, the last desire of wretches,
   Advancing their perdition-branded foreheads
   Like Envy's issue, or a bed of snakes.
BLACK BISHOP'S PAWN
   [*In the bag*] See, all's confounded, the game's lost, King's
                                                      taken. 185

179–219 Omitted in A. 'The bag' was apparently the traditional 'hell mouth',
   making the allegory obvious. A passage from one of the dispatches of
   the Spanish Ambassador to the Duke of Olivares provides a clue to the
   staging: 'The Prince of Wales . . . beat and kicked . . . Gondomar into
   Hell, which consisted of a great hole with hideous figures.' Edward M.
   Wilson and Olga Turner, 'The Spanish Protest Against *A Game at
   Chesse*', *Modern Language Review*, XLIV (1949), 477.

FAT BISHOP
   [In the bag] The White House has given us the bag, I
                                          thank 'em.

JESTING PAWN
   [In the bag] They had need have given you a whole bag by
                                         yourself.
   'Sfoot, this Fat Bishop has so squelched and squeezed me,
   So overlaid me, I have no verjuice left in me;
   You shall find all my goodness, an you look for 't,   190
   In the bottom of the bag.

FAT BISHOP   Thou malapert Pawn!
   The Bishop must have room, he will have room,
   And room to lie at pleasure.

JESTING PAWN   All the bag, I think,
   Is room too scant for your Spalato paunch.

BLACK BISHOP'S PAWN
   Down, viper of our order! Art thou showing   195
   Thy impudent whorish front?

BLACK QUEEN'S PAWN   Yes, monster-holiness.

WHITE KNIGHT
   Contention in the pit! Is hell divided?

WHITE KING
   You'd need have some of majesty and power
   To keep good rule amongst you: make room, Bishop.

            [Puts BLACK KING *into the bag]*

FAT BISHOP
   I'm not so easily moved when I'm once set,   200
   I scorn to stir for any King on earth.

WHITE QUEEN
   Here comes the Queen; what say you then to her?

           [Puts BLACK QUEEN *into the bag]*

FAT BISHOP
   Indeed a Queen may make a Bishop stir.

WHITE KNIGHT
   Room for the mightiest Machiavel-politician
   That e'er the devil hatched of a nun's egg.   205

186 *given us the bag* cheated us
187–191 lineation ed.
188 *'Sfoot* God's foot
189 *verjuice* ed. Vergis T acid liquor got from crab-apples
190 *an* (i.e., if) ed. and T
191 *malapert* impertinent
192–193 *room . . . paunch* puns on Rome (pronounced 'room')

[Puts BLACK KNIGHT *into the bag]*

FAT BISHOP
    He'll peck a hole in the bag and get out shortly
    But I'm sure I shall be the last creeps out,
    And that's the misery of greatness ever.
    Foh, your politician is not sound i' the vent,
    I smell him hither.   210

WHITE DUKE
    Room for a sun-burnt, tansy-faced beloved,
    An olive-coloured Ganymede, and that's all
    That's worth the bagging.

[Puts BLACK DUKE *into the bag]*

FAT BISHOP   Crowd in all you can,
    The Bishop will be still uppermost man,
    Maugre King, Queen, or politician.   215

WHITE KING
    So, now let the bag close, the fittest womb
    For treachery, pride and malice, whilst we, winner-like,
    Destroying, through heaven's power, what would destroy,
    Welcome our White Knight with loud peals of joy.

Epilogue

WHITE QUEEN'S PAWN

My mistress, the White Queen, hath sent me forth
And bade me bow thus low to all of worth
That are true friends of the White House and cause,
Which she hopes most of this assembly draws.
For any else, by envy's mark denoted,   5
To those night glow-worms in the bag devoted,
Where'er they sit, stand, and in corners lurk,
They'll be soon known by their depraving work.
But she's assured what they'd commit to bane,
Her White friends' loves will build up fair again.   10

211 *tansy-faced* yellow-faced
212 *Ganymede* minion, favourite
215 *Maugre* despite

211–212 'Olive-coloured' is the clearest indication in the play of the identity
    of the Black Duke, the Duke of Olivares. As to 'beloved' and 'Gany-
    mede', see note on Induction, 55–59 and F. H. Wilson, *King James VI
    and I* (London, 1959), pp. 383–386.
Epilogue. Omitted in A.

ADDITIONAL NOTES

Various other texts of the play precede the Prologue with the following prefatory material not found in T:

Title Page

Q1 and Q2 have an engraved title page with a double picture divided by a line. The upper frame shows eight characters from the play seated around a chess board. The lower frame shows the Fat Bishop, the Black Knight and the White Knight in a composite scene from the play.

Q3 has an engraved title page, obviously adapted from that of the other Qq, in which the upper frame and the figure of the White Knight in the lower are omitted and the Fat Bishop and Black Knight enlarged to fill the vacant space.

The figures in the lower frame of Q1 and Q2 are obvious likenesses of de Dominis, Gondomar, and Charles. The figures around the board may also have been intended to be likenesses, as follows: White and Black Kings and Queens: the sovereigns of England and Spain; White Duke: Buckingham; Black Duke: Olivares; White Bishop: Archbishop Abbot of Canterbury. See John Robert Moore, 'The Contemporary Significance of Middleton's *Game at Chesse*', *PMLA*, L (1935), 61–63.

The Picture Plainly Explained after the Manner of the Chess Play

Opposite the title page of Q1 and Q2 appears a poem with this title, as follows:

> A game at chess is here displayed,
> Between the Black and White House made,
> Wherein crown-thirsting policy,
> For the Black House, by fallacy,
> To the White Knight check often gives,
> And to some straits him thereby drives;
> The Fat Black Bishop helps also
> With faithless heart to give the blow:
> Yet, maugre all their craft, at length
> The White Knight, with wit-wondrous strength,
> And circumspective prudency,

Gives check-mate by discovery
To the Black Knight; and so at last
The game thus won, the Black House cast
Into the bag, and therein shut,
Find all their plumes and coxcombs cut.
 Plain dealing thus, by wisdom's guide,
 Defeats the cheats of craft and pride.

This poem is probably not by Middleton, for it appears to have been written by someone who was ignorant of chess and who was misled by the scene on the title page of Q1 and Q2 into misinterpreting the ending of the play.

To the Worthily-Accomplished Mr. William Hammond

In M, following the title page, appear verses with this title. as follows:

This, which nor stage, nor stationer's stall can show
(The common eye may wish for, but ne'er know),
Comes in its best love with the New Year forth,
As a fit present to the Hand of Worth.

The lines are in Middleton's hand, and the manuscript was obviously designed as a New Year's gift.

DRAMABOOKS

MD 37 *Platonov* by Anton Chekhov
MD 38 *Ugo Betti: Three Plays* (The Inquiry, Goat Island, The Gambler)
MD 39 *Jean Anouilh* Vol. 3 (Thieves' Carnival, Medea, Cécile, Traveler Without Luggage, The Orchestra, Episode in the Life of an Author, Catch As Catch Can)
MD 101 *Bussy D'Ambois* by George Chapman
MD 102 *The Broken Heart* by John Ford
MD 103 *The Duchess of Malfi* by John Webster
MD 104 *Doctor Faustus* by Christopher Marlowe
MD 105 *The Alchemist* by Ben Jonson
MD 106 *The Jew of Malta* by Christopher Marlowe
SD 1 *The Last Days of Lincoln* by Mark Van Doren
SD 2 *Oh Dad, Poor Dad, Mamma's Hung You in the Closet and I'm Feelin' So Sad* by Arthur Kopit
SD 3 *The Chinese Wall* by Max Frisch
SD 4 *Billy Budd* by Louis O. Coxe and Robert Chapman
SD 5 *The Devils* by John Whiting
SD 6 *The Firebugs* by Max Frisch
SD 7 *Andorra* by Max Frisch
SD 8 *Balm in Gilead and Other Plays* by Lanford Wilson
SD 9 *Matty and the Moron and Madonna* by Herbert Lieberman
SD 10 *The Brig* by Kenneth H. Brown
SD 11 *The Cavern* by Jean Anouilh
SD 12 *Saved* by Edward Bond
SD 13 *Eh?* by Henry Livings

CRITICISM

D 1 *Shakespeare and the Elizabethans* by Henri Fluchère
D 2 *On Dramatic Method* by Harley Granville-Barker
D 3 *George Bernard Shaw* by G. K. Chesterton
D 4 *Paradox of Acting* by Diderot and *Masks or Faces?* by William Archer
D 5 *The Scenic Art* by Henry James
D 6 *Preface to Hamlet* by Harley Granville-Barker
D 7 *Hazlitt on Theatre* ed. by William Archer and Robert Lowe
D 8 *The Fervent Years* by Harold Clurman
D 9 *The Quintessence of Ibsenism* by Bernard Shaw
D 10 *Papers on Playmaking* ed. by Brander Matthews
D 11 *Papers on Acting* ed. by Brander Matthews
D 12 *The Theatre* by Stark Young
D 13 *Immortal Shadows* by Stark Young
D 14 *Shakespeare: A Survey* by E. K. Chambers
D 15 *The English Dramatic Critics* ed. by James Agate
D 16 *Japanese Theatre* by Faubion Bowers
D 17 *Shaw's Dramatic Criticism* (1895-98) ed. by John F. Matthews
D 18 *Shaw on Theatre* ed. by E. J. West
D 19 *The Book of Job as a Greek Tragedy* by Horace Meyer Kallen
D 20 *Molière: The Man Seen Through the Plays* by Ramon Fernandez
D 21 *Greek Tragedy* by Gilbert Norwood
D 22 *Samuel Johnson on Shakespeare* ed. by W. K. Wimsatt, Jr.
D 23 *The Poet in the Theatre* by Ronald Peacock
D 24 *Chekhov the Dramatist* by David Magarshack
D 25 *Theory and Technique of Playwriting* by John Howard Lawson
D 26 *The Art of the Theatre* by Henri Ghéon
D 27 *Aristotle's Poetics* with an Introduction by Francis Fergusson
D 28 *The Origin of the Theater* by Benjamin Hunningher
D 29 *Playwrights on Playwriting* ed. by Toby Cole
D 30 *The Sense of Shakespeare's Sonnets* by Edward Hubler
D 31 *The Development of Shakespeare's Imagery* by Wolfgang Clemen
D 32 *Stanislavsky on the Art of the Stage* trans. by David Magarshack
D 33 *Metatheatre: A New View of Dramatic Form* by Lionel Abel
D 34 *The Seven Ages of the Theatre* by Richard Southern
D 35 *The Death of Tragedy* by George Steiner
D 36 *Greek Comedy* by Gilbert Norwood
D 37 *Ibsen: Letters and Speeches* ed. by Evert Sprinchorn
D 38 *The Testament of Samuel Beckett* by J. Jacobsen and W. R. Mueller
D 39 *On Racine* by Roland Barthes
D 40 *American Playwrights on Drama* ed. by Horst Frenz
D 41 *How Shakespeare Spent the Day* by Ivor Brown
D 42 *Brecht on Theatre* ed. by John Willett
D 43 *Costume in the Theatre* by James Laver
D 102 *Theatre: Volume II* ed. by Barry Hyams